ENNOBLE
FOR SUCCESS

From Civil War to a US CFO

Discover Wisdom-Filled Lessons to Support You in Living an Ennobled, Empowered and Positive Life

Dr. Kasthuri Henry, *PhD, CTP*

WHAT PEOPLE ARE SAYING

"This autobiography is a gem from start to finish. When describing this book, the word 'inspirational' is inadequate."
—Bob Whipple "The Trust Ambassador" MBA CPTD, CEO Leadergrow, Inc.

"[Dr. Henry] and her life will become ennobling catalysts for those who are lucky enough to read this book."
—Dr. Marina Kostina, CEO & Founder of Ravenous Life Healing Center

"Ennobled for Success is already one of the greatest gifts of the decade, offering exhilarating story-telling and fascinating 'chin check moments' for the student in all of us."
—Marquell Oliver, Founder of Pure Alchemy

"This is a heartfelt and transparent 'love letter' to those who feel they are not good enough."
—Traci S. Campbell, CEO & Founder, BIBO Worldwide, LLC & The BIBO Foundation.

"Dr. Kas crosses the chasm between war-torn persecuted Sri Lankan and successful, polished US business executive."
—Charlotte Allen, CEO, International Bestselling Author, Speaker

"A must-read for all who aspire to live this one life fully and without regret."
—Dr. Susila Kulasingam, Pharmaceutical Physician Executive and long-time friend.

"Ennobled for Success is a powerful book where every word hits home, inviting readers to reflect on their own life journey."
—Rennu Dhillon D.S.c., Founder – Genius Kids & Win With Words, Author and Motivational Speaker.

"Dr. Henry is a trustful humanitarian who cultivates her garden of life through her selfless love of other individuals' success. THIS BOOK IS A MUST-READ AND RE-READ!!!"
—Fire Chief Michael F. Spain, MA (Retired), Bensenville Fire Protection District

"Ennobled for Success is a must-read guide that will unleash the potential of any leader who wants to reach higher."
—Jacqueline Camacho-Ruiz, 21x Author, International Speaker, Entrepreneur, Pilot

"In a business world where one is so easily lost in the rat race, it is easy to be swept away. Ennobled for Success reminded me to be me, again. "
—Tara DeGrace

"[Dr. Kas] makes us believe that we can each develop the necessary noble qualities to attain our success by committing to the process of embracing gratitude!"
—Ruchira Palliyaguru, International Cricket Umpire, Sri Lanka Cricket and International Cricket Council

"In our present day and age, it is more important than ever that leaders be held accountable for developing and spreading noble qualities."
—Patrick Haddad, CEO Oopgo Inc, Forbes Tech Council Expert Advisor, and USMC Veteran

"As a world-renowned expert profiler who understands how people are wired, I recognize Dr. Kasthuri's brilliance in helping you go deeper to bring the best of you forward."
—Susan Ibitz, Human Behavior Hacker, Human Behavior Lab

KASTHURI HENRY | 5

"**Students, teachers, and business leaders will all benefit from the delightful fruits of knowledge that grow in Dr Kas' garden.**"
—Wolfgang Trampe, Human Resources Leader, Duracell (A Berkshire Hathaway Company), Latin America

"**While some use fables, Kas shares real-life experiences to teach how being authentic, caring, and purpose-driven can bring success.**"
—Joe Schum, Division Chief – Truckee Meadows Fire & Rescue, Reno, NV and International Public Safety Leadership Ethics Institute (IPSLEI) Board Member

Ennobled for Success:
From Civil War to a US CFO

RHG Media Productions
25495 Southwick Drive #103
Hayward, CA 94544.

ISBN 978-1-7359555-0-6 (paperback)
ISBN 978-1-7359555-1-3 (hardcover)

Visit us on line at www.YourPurposeDrivenPractice.com

Printed in the United States of America.

All Images included in this book were created and are owned by the author.

CONTENTS

INTRODUCTION

In my quiet moments, I look back at my life's journey and recall the countless everyday people who have made my life possible—the ordinary people in different countries and cities who were rich in humanity, who cared about another person with absolutely no expectation in return. Everyday heroes from all walks of life armed with selfless compassion and pure kindness made a difference in my life. They have taught me that *I do not have to save the world; I must simply be mindful of saving a person so that a whole world of possibilities opens for that individual.*

When I share snippets of my life story with others, be it in a classroom to illustrate a point, during one of my speaking engagements, on my radio show, or a casual conversation, I am told that I ought to write a book. However, writing about me has always seemed a bit too self-serving. One day, on a flight home after a business trip, during my introspective moment, it occurred to me that I should write but write for a larger purpose. By sharing my evolution as a being, I could thank the noble souls who shaped my path; write as a way to celebrate them. Dolly Parton's song "Coat of Many Colors" evokes deep emotions in me because it reminds me of the tapestry of my own life. A rich life woven by individuals who dared to love me and lift me up to where I am today. A tapestry that embodies their goodness. A tapestry that always warms my heart regardless of the dark clouds hovering over me on any given day. A tapestry that proves to me that daring to care and being kind is the cornucopia of eternal wealth we can pass on. It is my hope that by sharing pivotal moments of my journey as it shaped me, would help others be introspective and pause to honor their own everyday heroes. Honor those who have lived a rich life of purpose, to give of themselves for the betterment of others. This is truly a moment to celebrate our faith in humanity, unconditional love for fellow travelers, and compassion for those around us. At a time when our world appears to be harsher, let us celebrate goodness that lives amongst us.

We are each born as beings, and somewhere along in life, we stop seeing ourselves as beings and start defining ourselves by what we do. My life journey has taught me that the being that I am is who I truly am, and my being shapes all my doing. I am larger than what I do, and I cannot allow myself to be defined by my job, my title, or what I do for a living.

- **Introducing Myself (My Being)**: I am a compassionate human being who believes everyone should have the opportunity to fulfill their life's purpose and live an authentic life fearlessly with the right to not be defined by a single story.

- **Introducing What I Do (My Doing)**: I am an accomplished professional who trains organizations and coaches individuals across the world to grow with mindfulness, demonstrating good governance to balance the interest of the individual, organization, and society for sustained mutual prosperity.

  The distinction has a difference. The choices I have made in life, while difficult and unimaginable at times, have forced me to weigh who I am and choose based on the being that I am. Those who have shaped me taught me two priceless lessons: the importance of ennobling and embracing gratitude, two ingredients that have laid the foundation for my success.

- **Ennobling**: In my doctoral dissertation that focused on the nexus of profits and ethics for organizational viability, I define ennobling as the process through which noble qualities are developed to spawn mindful leaders capable of embracing good governance. Both in the Western and Eastern philosophies, noble qualities are not relegated to nobility. Noble qualities of kindness, caring, compassion, empathy, sense of duty, doing the right thing, being selfless, leaving a place better than you find it, etc., can be developed by individuals. **This development process requires**:

o Deep self-reflection

o Ability to see the micro-messages and subtext in situations through acute self-awareness and social awareness

o Mindfulness to recognize the invisible people of everyday life who have the potential to shape us beyond our wildest dreams, if we just allow it

o Being in the moment to embrace life with all senses— so seeing with the heart, smiling with the eyes, and willing to engage the soul is possible

o Having the courage to be vulnerable and taking the chance of getting hurt while keeping the faith that goodness dwells everywhere

o Embodying hope without reservation that the universe is rigged in our favor, knowing hope is not a strategy but an endless source of inspiration.

• *Embracing Gratitude*: I grew up in a very conservative, traditional Hindu home in a culture and society that was diverse and respectful of gender identities, religious philosophies, and understood the transformational value of sound education and good health. This meant there were inherent contradictions to grapple with, as a female child who could be vocal and well-read in society while being restricted within the household. This was not an easy place to be. It caused confusion and, at times, anger inside me. Reading became one of my two refuges. Engaging in deep discussion with everyday people was the other. Society respected intellectual explorations, and it was not relegated to the educated elite, which made the everyday invisible people around me my wellspring. I saw them, and they saw me. My parents never noticed me talking and engaging with the driver, cleaning lady, storekeeper, fisherman, bus conductor, or the baker. They had wisdom no book could impart, and they had the noble qualities I needed to learn.

One day, when I was around ten years old, my father sat me down to teach me facts of life as he saw it. I went through puberty at ten, and he thought that meant I was ready to be an adult and carry the full responsibility of womanhood. He started getting frustrated when I continued to challenge his notions. I had a way of making my parents lose their cool with my logic, so much so that my mother referred to me as the "judge advocate general." Physically punishing children was commonplace in the culture, and asking sons to beat up daughters to make daughters conform within the conservative households was also normal, at least in my home. I never took that as a way of life and soon taught my brothers and adults in the family what would happen if they touched me. I had learned to defend myself and could muster strength by channeling my anger. I was never proud of that seething anger, but it only got unleased when I or others around me were threatened.

In his frustration, father decided to lay down the law by saying, "You owe your life to me because my seed gave you this life. Everything you are, everything you do, and everything you accomplish is because of me. I own you. You do what I tell you to do."

Even at ten years of age, that did not sit well with me. Keeping my mouth shut for fear of being beaten was not my style. I responded, "Father, it is true that this body, the physical presence, is a product of your seed. So, go ahead and do what you may to this body you claim you own. But, never for a moment forget that the soul inside my body comes from my maker, my God. I will never let you own my soul. My soul will help me live my life on my terms. You nor anyone else will ever be able to touch it. I am not this body. I am the soul within."

My words came rushing out, mixed with anger and determination while daring him to get harsh. He knew he had pushed me to the edge, where he was not going to get through to me that day. While that day ended for him, like any other day trying to fit me into a box he believed I should be in, I was having none of it. Ever! That was the day I fully realized the power of gratitude. The gratitude for all the invisible people who showed me the lessons of life; gratitude for the books and wisdom left by those who came before me to shape my thinking; gratitude for the God who gave me the determination and intangible powers to fearlessly stand up and speak my truth, as a child. I realized that my life is a special gift of God and what I do with it is my gift of gratitude to my maker and all those who shape me in countless ways. My age, my gender, my looks, my station in life, nothing eclipsed the being that I was. **I was my soul, and that soul needed to live a life of gratitude to fulfill its purpose and be ennobled for success.**

I started keeping a journal. I cataloged what went on in my life and how it was shaping me. I knew then that I would be a writer, and my writing would focus on inspiring others like I was inspired. All my writing was in Tamil, my native language indigenous to the South Asian subcontinent. I share the translated template of my journal in English here for the benefit of anyone else who wants to keep a gratitude journal. Keeping a gratitude journal has been an important part of my journey; embracing lessons and staying grateful were key to finding my balance in life. I recommend keeping a daily gratitude journal to support you in living a life of gratitude. Here is a sample structure you can use for your journal and daily reflections.

What Happened	How It Impacted Me	Why I Am Grateful

©Dr. Kasthuri Henry, *Ennobled for Success*

The Gratitude Journal which accompanies this book will be released on Amazon. The fifty-two-week writing journal will help facilitate the transformational journey of those who choose to adopt this ennobled road to success.

The more I felt grateful, the more I was able to handle my anger and negative emotions swirling within me. I started becoming curious as to why. As I grew older and started being introduced to biology and sciences as an early teenager, I started learning how the sense of gratitude truly influenced the brain chemistry and gave me a superpower to thrive in spite of my circumstances. Being a visual thinker, I had the image in my mind, based on my readings, how gratitude helped me rewire my brain function. Over the years, that visualization has been refined. I share my visualization here with the intent to help others benefit from my learnings.

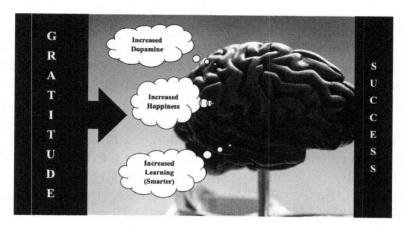

Adapted from *Psychology Today*,
Dr. Kasthuri Henry, © *Ennobled for Success*

Sri Lanka, the island nation that gave birth to the word "serendipity," is my birthplace: a picturesque island blessed with emerald mountains, cascading waterfalls, pristine beaches, magnificent wildlife, wondrous nature, and a community that cared about its neighbors. This land of eternal summer did, however, have its dark side. The post-colonial strife and the resulting public policies dividing the people for the enrichment of politicians did not escape my motherland. I grew up in a world that was wonderful and cruel at the same time. Wonderful in so many little ways and yet cruel in so much societal strife, both within families and communities. It is in this intersection of sheer goodness and utter evil that my life journey began many moons ago.

In the interest of providing context to the vignettes you are about to read, it is imperative that I provide you with some much-needed background.

Brief history of Sri Lanka and the thirty-year civil war

The Sri Lankan civil war was a modern-day post-colonial strife, no different from other civil wars that ensued at the end of colonial regimes across the world. Our civil war was for land. When the British left the island in 1948, they left an island comprising of multiple kingdoms as a single nation. The two major inhabitants of Sri Lanka are Tamil Hindus and Sinhala Buddhists. To understand the civil war, one has to understand the island and the history of its people. Tamils were the affluent minority the British handpicked and transported across the colonies as their administrators. While Indians were brought into the island to work the tea plantations, they never enslaved the Sri Lankans. However, they segregated the Tamils from the Sinhalese, thus transporting Tamil and the Hindu culture across Africa, the Caribbean, South America, and Europe.

Tamil is a Dravidian language native to the South Asian subcontinent, and scholars believe that the Indus Valley Civilization was Dravidian, pre-dating Indo-Aryan languages from which Sinhala evolved.[I] Tamil is spoken in many countries and is one of the official languages of modern India (Tamil Nadu, a South Indian State of Tamil People), Singapore, and more. Today, Tamil is one of the oldest languages in the world.[II]

Sinhala language and Buddhism came into Sri Lanka, where Tamil Hindus were already present in their Dravidian land. The Tamil and the Sinhala communities occupied different kingdoms with integration through arranged marriages. Both groups looked alike and worshiped the same Gods. The only difference was their mother tongue. Portuguese first colonized parts of the island between 1505–1658, followed by the Dutch between 1658–1796, and England between 1796–1948. England was the only one to occupy the whole island toward the latter half of its colonial period.[III] We were called Ceylon during this period of European colonization.

Upon independence in 1948, as the new Sri Lanka emerged, nationalism became important and English education was abolished to be replaced by compulsory mother-tongue education. This language-based segregation, as people learned in different classrooms and populations segregated in their language clusters, was the seedling for the civil war to come.

Tamils were a minority population in a single-nation island, and the majority Sinhala population was in political power in the Parliamentary system established in 1947–1948. Political instability and rising nationalism of the 1950s and 1960s shaped what Sri Lanka was to become.[IV]

I remember as a child when the election took place every four years, my father's bank placed security in our home, and my mother's school—run by Catholic nuns—took my mother and the four children in so we could live in the infirmary with the nuns. This was a safety precaution the island had adopted because while the two major parties run by Sinhala Buddhist groups competed for power, the Tamil Hindu population, the largest minority, was the swing vote that determined the outcome. It was common for the losing party to harm Tamil families, burn the homes and businesses of Tamil people, and subject the minority to their anger. Increasingly, the conservative Buddhist monks and institutions started promoting anti-Tamil rhetoric with conservative politicians wanting Sri Lanka to be a Sinhala Buddhist nation. There were no Sinhala Buddhists anywhere else in the world, and they believed that the island should be theirs and theirs alone.

I grew up in Colombo, the business and political capital of the island that was diverse and cosmopolitan with European, Persian, and Chinese descendants peacefully living in economic prosperity, aided by international trade. These communities had marriages with one another, and the adults had grown up in the British colonial period with English education. My parents were a part of this educated urban community with friends and colleagues from all the ethnic groups. Growing up as children in the 1970s, we did not fear our neighbors and friends. However, we never were in a classroom with Sinhala children. The Muslim (Persian descendants) and Burger (Portuguese, Dutch, and English descendants) children had to choose to study in either Sinhala or Tamil.

The civil war that erupted in July 1983 following the slow burn leading up to it was instrumental in shaping my perspectives and how I would approach life as an adult. In the following chapters, you will be introduced to how situations and people shaped me to become who I am today. I want to take a moment and share with you who I am today and what I have accomplished to help you keep the triumph over obstacles in perspective. Being a thirteen-year-old refugee child in my own country was not my story. I refuse to be defined by a single story, as that is how stereotypes are created. My story is one of resilience, tenacity, courage, and overcoming all the negativity that surrounds a senseless war. I worked at identifying, understanding and dealing with anger, hate, fear, and shame; focused on embracing happiness and peace through a grateful heart.

BRIEF SNAPSHOT OF TODAY

I became a regional Chief Financial Officer in a Fortune-500 company in my early thirties: feat for a woman in the United States. I had earned my MBA and was invited to teach US military and public safety leadership as a visiting professor to shape financial strategy and decision-making while being a young CFO. I have been teaching this group of professionals in the areas of fiscal aspects, data analysis, and leadership, while carrying a US military clearance to enter the bases—an accomplishment that cannot be put into words for a young girl who lived as a Sri Lankan Tamil fleeing the atrocities of government military. I was inducted into the 2005 AFP300 by the Association of Financial Professionals for being an international finance leader. I was recognized as *Financial Executive of the Year* in 2007 by The Institute of Management Accountants.

I went on to earn my PhD in finance and become the Chief Financial Officer for a $22-billion-dollar pension fund with $11 billion in assets to bring about business transformation through organizational and regulatory changes. I am the founder and CEO of my firm, KasHenry Inc., focusing on consulting, training, and coaching to shape global businesses and leaders. I have overseen the acquisition of a major global brand Duracell by a Fortune-100 Company, Berkshire Hathaway owned by the Oracle of Omaha Mr. Warren Buffet, and implemented post-acquisition integration, training, and development to unleash the deal value over a five-year strategy.

Today, I am a financial business strategist, award-winning graduate school professor, award-winning author, thought leader, motivational speaker, host of a podcast, and award-winning mentor committed to shaping an inclusive future of equity. I host my podcast, "Unleash Your Inner Goldilocks: How to Get It Just Right," to take my message of positive social change across the world and showcase change agents who are catalysts for positive transformation. These are my accomplishments based on what I do, fully influenced by who I truly am.

The person I have become is far more important compared to the accomplishments. I have a happy twenty-two-year marriage with my best friend, transcending race, religion, ethnicity, language, and all else that are superficial. I continue to demonstrate the courage to be kind and inspire others to rise above their circumstances. *Building to last and ennobling for success* is my life mission. I value peace and happiness above all material things. I value people and know that things are to be used to aid a fruitful life while living in a world where things are valued, and people are used. Lasting impactful relationships nurture me; they are my true treasures.

I have a long journey ahead, and it is with unbridled hope fueled by gratitude that I wake up to face each day. I am aware that what I seek will seek me, congruent with the laws of the universe. Staying rooted in kindness, demonstrating empathy, and daring to care is what I strive to embody. Success is not a destination. It is a journey. A journey that builds with each step and each breath.

CHAPTER 1

LISTENING, GIVING OTHERS THEIR VOICE

"First duty of love is to listen."
—Paul Tillich

I was born the oldest daughter and the second of four children, in a traditional Hindu household, and my earliest memories were about knowing duty and responsibility. As children, our duty was to obey our parents and learn; as the oldest daughter, my duty was to be the responsible one with the siblings. We lived in a second-story rental apartment in Colombo, and the ground-floor garage of our unit was occupied by a rickshaw. A rickshaw is an old fashioned non-mechanized mode of transportation where the passengers sat in a canopied seat high up while the driver picked up the long handles and ran to get his passengers to their destination. We had our own rickshaw, and the driver Thevar, an older man who had the kindest eyes and warmest of hearts, was my best friend and hero. Thevar in Tamil, my native tongue, and one of the oldest languages in the world,[1] means "saint." Thevar definitely lived up to his name in my book. I adored him, and he made me feel like a princess in a world where there were no princesses.

I remember as a two-and-a-half-year-old wanting to go to Montessori School because my older brother was being sent there while I stayed at home with my two younger siblings and the live-in help. At a young age, I had the drive and desire to learn. I could not accept my parents telling me "no" or "not yet." Having had all of us kids in their forties, my parents did not quite understand how to communicate with young children, and I was not making it any easier with my insistent questioning. Their responses of, "We will tell you when you can go," or, "Not yet," were not acceptable to me, especially since I was the oldest girl responsible for the younger ones while they were at work. In my childish mind, when they repeatedly said I was the oldest daughter, and therefore, the responsible one, I took it rather seriously. That meant I was in charge. If I was in charge and I was responsible, then why I could not go to Montessori School was a huge puzzle. It did not occur to me that the live-in help was the adult in the home, and I was being taught a consistent lesson in duty through this parental message. Looking back, it is quite obvious that I took my duty seriously and decided to hit the ground running.

As soon as my parents had left for work and Thevar took my brother in the rickshaw to Montessori School, I got dressed and walked to the Montessori School. I had, on previous occasions, talked Thevar into taking me for a ride around the neighborhood and figured how to get to my planned destination. Blessed with a keen sense of direction, I mean physical direction—although one could argue I probably acted like I had my life direction also figured out in the way I carried on—I arrived in school. To this day, it escapes me as to why the school did not immediately contact my parents, but instead, they allowed me to attend class. I must have been convincing in my explanation of being ready to learn. After all, how many two-and-a-half-year-olds walk into a school and announce themselves as being ready to learn?

After an exciting day of learning, I was walking home with a skip in my step when Thevar confronted me with his rickshaw and told me that everyone at home was looking for me. I paid absolutely no attention to why people would be looking for me and instead hopped on to the rickshaw for my ride home and shared my exciting first day at school with Thevar. He was so happy for me and was proud of my initiative to accomplish what my heart desired. I was on cloud nine, and then, with a thud, this euphoric high of having accomplished something came crashing down. My mom was angry and upset all at the same time, and the assumption all adults had made were either I ran away from home, or I had been kidnapped. No one would listen to my exciting day. Everyone was ready with their own version of a lecture to make me listen and live in a manner they had all decided my life ought to be lived. My mom somehow managed to deliver her lecture to me amidst her weeping. I remember thinking that none of the grown-ups had any sense of adventure, except for Thevar. As if he heard me think out loud, he gave me a handful of candy and winked to let me know I was not this horrible, ungrateful child everyone else was accusing me of because I did not wait to be told what and when to do things.

That was the first moment of my life lesson—a lesson that most adults have their own way of approaching life, and to them, right versus wrong will always be black or white. While this lesson has proved out to be true throughout my adult life, today, I do understand the fright I gave my mom when she came home after her teaching to find out I was not home, and no one knew where I was. However, at that time, I missed the sense of adventure and the need to celebrate that free spirit; I felt unfairly scolded for taking my duty to learn rather seriously and having my own mind to pursue my duty in the only way available to me. I also did not appreciate that all the adults were blind to different perspectives, especially my perspective because I had one and thought it was worthy of being heard if they had not already heard it through my insistent probing about starting school.

The next day, there was no argument if I could go to school because everyone knew I would go with or without permission, and therefore, the best course of action was to send me to school in the rickshaw. Thus began my daily rides to Montessori School. Thevar took me to school along with his other kids, and then he picked me up after school. I now had my hero to talk to about all the things running through my mind. He was open to discussing any topic my little heart desired and shared his wisdom with me. I loved our chats and looked forward to them every morning and afternoon. Thevar understood me like no one else did, and he guided me in ways that helped me in my impressionable young life. He definitely had an extra special soft spot for me because he bought me little treats every day to show me he cared and listened to me with great patience. He was the only person who listened to me and engaged in a meaningful conversation with me. Through him, I learned the importance of listening and demonstrating unconditional love and acceptance by listening, for listening gives the other person's voice meaning and value. Not being heard is to forcefully make another lose their voice, and I wanted to grow up to be like Thevar, a kind and caring human being who made time to listen and engage in meaningful dialogue by giving others their own voice.

Today, as an educator and practitioner, I have ample opportunities to take a moment and listen to those around me. I am the professor, and business leader individuals gravitate toward when they feel the need to talk to someone. When I am approached for a conversation, I send a silent prayer of gratitude to Thevar and the beauty of his soul for teaching me the importance of just stopping everything else and listening without any filters with the sole purpose of giving another soul their space to be. I not only learned to listen to the words spoken, but I also learned the art of nonverbal communication as a means of giving comfort to those who need it. The countless ways Thevar and I spoke to each other over the years, when society insisted he had his place, and I had mine due to our different stations in societal status, helped me develop the skill of talking without words. The universe sent me the best teacher when I needed it, and who says teachers are only in the classrooms? **Life is filled with teachable and learnable moments if we just open our hearts and souls to give the universe a fighting chance.**

It is vital to understand that 70 percent of all communication is nonverbal,[2] and when we only half-listen to others talking in the name of multitasking, we are barely absorbing the 30 percent of all verbal communication. **There is a distinctive difference between listening and hearing. Hearing, to me, is the mere registering of sound devoid of the meaning. Listening, on the other hand, comes from active engagement with the intent to comprehend the words and body language while seeking to understand.** Today, I see so much talking and not enough listening all around me, at work and in society; it does not surprise me that we have so much anger, hate, and misunderstandings resulting in toxic human environments. For some reason, we have stopped listening to each other, and we have stopped listening to our own inner voice.

Life requires listening to our inner self and listening to those around us because we all impact each other, whether we want to or not. **Listening is an act of respect and love, leading to understanding.** Love and respect start from within because we can never give to others what we do not have for ourselves. **Actions stemming from understanding do not divide but unite and do not hurt but heal. Therefore, listening is one of the fundamental building blocks of a leader, a person who develops the ability to command respect and following of others.** Everything I am today stems from my ability to listen and give others the ability to find their voice because one man gave me the gift of developing my personal voice and thought. Thevar's actions showed me the art of truly listening so I could have a sense of belonging. When I felt a sense of belonging, I knew that I matter. When I channel him to truly listen, I am passing on his gift to others so that belonging and being worthy spread as his legacy long after his time on this earth.

Lessons Learned:

➢ **Listening is an important life skill** *that helps demonstrate that ideas and opinions of others matter.*

➢ **Listening is a leadership characteristic** *that helps create an inclusive environment rooted in respect, empowering others to rise up and live their full potential.*

➢ **Listening with the heart and keeping an open mind** *can bring about unimaginable life lessons from unexpected places.*

CHAPTER 2

I AM WHAT I BELIEVE

"The most important relationship is the
relationship with self and the divine within."
—Unknown

Like all post-colonial societies, ours in Sir Lanka was col-
or-conscious too. The color of the skin presented a silent
social desirability pecking order. One of my childhood memories was associated with my mom asking me on various
occasions why I came out dark in spite of her maintaining a
strict diet of all the foods necessary for giving birth to a light-
skinned child. One such food item is called "Kunkumam," a
flower that women supposedly eat so they could have fair-
skinned children. My mom had done it when she had conceived my older brother, and she had proof that it worked.

Then, I had come along and failed to adhere to the rules, even at birth. My little sister, on the other hand, was born a beautiful, light-skinned baby, making my mom happy and proud.

Being from a Hindu family also meant that my parents had to give dowry when I grew up so a man could marry me. In the marriage-broker-organized arranged marriage world, "Sons are a credit and daughters are a debit on the family balance sheet" was what I repeatedly heard at home. Now that I am a finance executive, I know that all assets are debits, and therefore daughters are the true assets of a family, but I did not have the heart to share this kernel of truth with my parents in their later years. Sons bring in dowry while daughters take away family wealth as dowry. This implied that my family would, at some point, break-even because we were two boys and two girls. Sons who become doctors and engineers command the highest dowry while fair maidens are considered beautiful and desirable in the matrimonial marketplace. Why I needed to know all this long before I was even six years old beats me, but I was made aware of it on a regular basis.

As a dark-skinned girl with a mind of her own who spoke her truth, my very presence was sufficient to scandalize my parents on any given day. As an acute listener of both verbal and nonverbal communication, I picked up quite a bit. Most of what I was picking up did not make any sense to me because they appeared to be ignorant on the face of it due to its absence of caring, compassion, or kindness. There were countless occasions where I heard my mom weeping at the altar, asking God, "Why couldn't Kasthuri have been a boy?" Like all children, this used to bother me in the beginning and to seek my own answers, I started reading.

I was lucky to be able to read, write, and speak Tamil, an old language, with an epic list of books spanning philosophy, literature, humanities, art, culture, and science. My parents were focused on education, like all Asian families, and we all had library cards by the time we could read. I could also take the bus and go to school or the library long before I was ten. I was responsible for taking my sister and myself to Holy Family Convent by bus, including crossing the main highway in Colombo, Galle Road. We also had a home filled with books that I loved. I become an avid reader, searching for answers amongst the printed words. Reading gave me the time to think, evaluate, and examine my thoughts. I started becoming rather introverted in a household that did not understand my physical or intellectual being.

There are many things I am thankful for, including the opportunity to read, learn, and when opportunities warranted debate. I am most of all, thankful for the names I was given at birth, consistent with the Hindu tradition. Each child has a horoscope prepared by the priest or spiritual leader at the temple, and this horoscope is so specific, it uses the longitude, latitude, and time of birth to build the chart. Based on this horoscope chart, I was given a Hindu name, "Vadivambikai," a manifestation of Goddess Shakti, who was said to be the beautiful goddess who destroys evil. My mom was completing her thesis on Gandhi's non-violence peace movement when she conceived me, and once she realized I was a girl, she named me "Kasthuri" after Gandhi's wife, giving me two names. Whenever I hear my mom asking God, "Why was she not a boy?" I wondered if she had hoped to have a son who would grow up and be like Gandhi. This made me read about Gandhi and his life work, his relationship with his wife Kasthuri, and his role in establishing a movement for civil rights through peaceful means that has since shaped iconic leaders such as Dr. Martin Luther King, Jr. and Nelson Mandela.[3] **The more I read, the more I realized I was going to be a great disappointment to my parents because I was never going to be the fair maiden who could bring them great pride through an arranged marriage as a desirable bride, and I was never going to live up to the mark Gandhi left on humanity; I was going to fail on both counts.**

However, my reading had already enlightened me that there is more than one avenue and more than one meaning to all things in life. So, I pursued my research into what other meanings "Kasthuri" embodied. Libraries are wonderful places for intellectual treasure hunts, and I found the treasure I was seeking, to my great delight. The name of the book or the author escapes my mind after all these years, but what I read has stayed with me. Kasthuri or Kasturi, whichever way it is spelled in English, was a type of deer roaming the Himalayan mountains. The male deer carries musk in its naval. This musk is an integral part of Ayurvedic medicine, traditional South Asian medicine employing nature's abundance to heal what ails human beings. In Ayurvedic medicine, this Kasthuri musk is used as the last resort to help save a life.[4]

The story that went along with this piece of medical information is what caught my undivided attention. The male deer runs and roams the Himalia region searching for the source of the fragrance without realizing from where the actual musk fragrance is emanating. As the end of life approaches and this particular male deer keels over and curls up to accept the inevitable death, he realized that he carried the fragrance within him all along. **The story ends with the message that a child named Kasthuri is intended to grow up with the knowledge that** *what was needed to succeed in life and live a life of meaning was already contained within themselves; all they had to do was first be aware of it and then develop the ability to draw from within.* I remember thinking to myself, *what a wonderful gift I was given by my parents, given a name that carries so much to help shape my future.* **My destiny was to be shaped by my names Vadivambikai Kasthuri, the beautiful goddess who destroys evil and who draws from within her soul all she needs to heal the world around her.**

Once I understood who I was, what I, as a soul, was potentially capable of, all the talk about my physical appearance and superficial skin color ceased to matter. I continued my research to learn about the science of skin and cultural differences with their approaches to color. I quickly understood that individuals with light skin pay good money to get tanned and look like me. Naturally a child with the gift of gab, I employed humor to combat color disparagement. I also developed the knack of getting people to look at the real me instead of the superficial surface because, after all, I am what is within my soul, and that is where I should draw from if I am truly Kasthuri. **What started off as a defensive exploration had turned into a proactive life mission that evolved into my own approach to life.**

Armed with all this information and new knowledge, I used it to debate my parents when they said anything that I felt was not nice. When my mom asked me, "Why did you not come out white?" I would counter that with, "Why did you not marry a white man?" and she would say, "What has that got to do with you?" and I would respond with, "You would have given me better odds at being light-skinned." This inevitably made my parents furious, and I would insist that "Dad is brown; I look exactly like him with brown skin; are you both not happy I did not come out bald like him?" Or, I would say, "At least we all have proof that I am my dad's daughter because I look exactly like him and have his skin color." I thought this was a comeback with humor, but no one else in the family got it. **To them, brown and bold was a bad combination for a girl, and no one was going to marry me. My personal mission was to keep all marriage proposals away because this traditional thinking of arranged marriage was not going to suit me.** I was not even ten years old yet!

I took my debating skills to school, too. Holy Family Convent, run by nuns, was one of the prestigious schools in Colombo, and I was the captain of my debating team. Much to my joy, the nuns picked the topic of "Arranged Marriage versus Love Marriage" for a final debate contest. Any guesses on which was assigned to my team? If you thought it was arranged marriage, you guessed wrong! I prepared with my team to argue for love marriage and carefully prepared my closing argument on factually destroying the basis for arranged marriage. **The exercise was more than a mere debate for me. It was my argument for my life as it was to evolve. I was planting the seedlings for my personal choices early in life because I was sick and tired of hearing at home how everything about**

me was wrong. I was going to make my case with facts and humor and move my audience to see my perspective. I knew I could convince my fellow classmates who were all Tamil girls in this all-girls convent school. I did not stop to think about how the nuns might react because what do they know about marriage, arranged or otherwise? Boy, was I wrong!

I delivered a fact-based opening argument, and my team-mates did their parts to build our case for love marriage and systematically challenge the foundation of an arranged marriage. Then came my closing argument. I paraphrase my Tamil debate words in English for the purpose of narrating this story.

"Arranged marriage is a brokered proposition where the girl pays the boy, and the bidding of multiple girls increases the dowry rate for the boy, creating an auction of the boy to the highest bidder. Once the highest-bidding girl gets the boy, the whole community comes to give their consent at the wedding, followed by the boy and girl engaging in post-marital sex because pre-marital relationships are not acceptable. For the sake of argument, let's look at what pros-titution would be like. Women are paraded in front of men, and each man picks the woman he wants, agreeing to pay the price for sex with her. There is no community blessing, but money changes hands in return for sex. Arranged marriage is, therefore, socially engineered, legalized prostitution of sons by parents. Any girl following tradition and committing to an arranged marriage is part of that prostitution ring because she engages in the same physical act with the purchased boy. Arranged marriages, therefore, are not moral and should be eliminated from our society. We do not need to condone legalized prostitution."

I went on to speak of love and its unconditional nature, its ability to unite humanity and heal all wounds, its inherent potential to bring peace and harmony into a home and family, and so much more. I doubt any of my teachers who them-selves were in arranged marriages or the nuns thought their star pupil had made a winning argument. The look I received was that I had just committed heresy.

My team won the debate, but that was not the highlight that followed. The nuns were saying their rosary to save my soul, and the other teachers planned how to talk some sense into me. What followed was a collective lecture. They unanimously felt that, as a natural leader of the class, I was attempting to lead all the young girls astray. I was supposed to use my knowledge and gift of gab to affirm the traditional message. Little did they know that I had years of experience dealing with such lectures. I confirmed to them that I understood their concerns and sincerely apologized for challenging their norms. I also asked them to look at it from a different perspective. The perspective of a young mind that used logic and asked if A = B and B = C, should it not be true that A = C? I was gently reminded that my math and logic skills are exceptional, but this is about life.

I never went home and shared this story with my family because my poor parents would have jumped off a cliff if they heard my closing argument. I knew what they did not know would not hurt them, especially in this instance. I also knew that no one would dare repeat my closing argument for fear of bad karma. It is not just the Catholics who instill guilt in their community. The Hindus got there first with karma. **I, however, had read on karma and knew that meant each action has a reaction; my thoughts, actions, and words matter, and they become my character. I was comfortable speaking my mind, and challenging norms that I felt were unfair.** After all, I did not want to end up in an arranged marriage to a boy who thought he could get more money because I was not light-skinned. I am deeper than my skin, and this was an argument for saving my soul from a fate worse than death. This was not a mere debate for me.

It's strange how a child's mind works. It is even stranger why such subject matters were used as discussion topics in my culture. Now that I live in the US, I realize that these are topics for university curriculum taught by those who have spent years specializing in difficult cultural and social norms. A middle school debate topic like this could get a US school system in such hot water, but in Sri Lanka, we took the approach of education preparing children for life. Prepared was what I was getting. Another thing I am very grateful for is my early education in Sri Lanka at a good school that helped me prepare for all aspects of life. It was as if the universe knew that I needed to go through these steps to grow into the adult I am today. All I needed to do was be a sponge while being open to the endless possibilities the universe offered.

Early education prepared me for learning how to learn, think critically, and ask probing questions until I got to the root of the matter at hand. Reading improved my vocabulary and made me a very good writer. Being multilingual with the ability to read, write, and speak three different languages, including English, opened a treasure trove of knowledge for my insatiable appetite. I realized that knowledge was the food for my soul. The various Tamil philosophy books and poetry I read affirmed that in this life journey, we are simply passing through. **The only things that come with me, the real me, my soul, at the end of this life, are:**

1. My knowledge

2. My karma resulting from my life and how I touch the lives of others

3. My soul's relationship with its maker

I learned that my body is a gift from my parents, but my soul, the very essence of who I am, is a gift from my God. I owe my soul to no one, and I need to live a life worthy of that gift from my God. I cannot allow anyone to guilt me into doing what they want from me, for my life is between my God and me. The only real way to show my gratitude to my maker is to live a life worthy of the gift given to me and lead with my soul.

Reading, introspection, and making my case without anger by speaking my truth have aided my life journey and brought me to where I am today. Everyone who tried to force me to conform, everyone who told me that I was not enough, everyone who put the superficial externalities ahead of the being that I truly am, have all made me the strong person I am today. **I am absolutely grateful to all these people who are family, teachers, and neighbors, for forcing me to find my inner self and calmly follow my path.** With their help and my tenacious determination, I was able to build a relationship with the divine within me, my soul.

"I am not this hair; I am not this skin,
I am the soul that lives within."
—Rumi

Today, as a professional in a male-dominated workplace, I am constantly asked how I became a young female CFO in the US before the age of thirty-five and what advice I have for other women and minorities. I will take a moment and share my usual response here with you. I do not see myself within the confines of gender or race. Not even in a specific color or ethnicity. I am not a single story and certainly not a story broad-brushed based on superficiality. Who I am stems from my soul; that soul is devoid of race, creed, color, gender, and all other things superficial. When I live my professional life from that place of universality, others meet me at that same place, if they have the capacity to do so. My professional life was made possible because good, hard-working businessmen of different ethnicities respected me and took a chance on me. They were not petty. They were not nasty. They were caring. They cared about both business success as well as mentoring me. I went on to become the boss of some of these men, but we always had that bond and utmost respect for each other because we saw each other as people with a shared purpose.

I have chosen to approach life as if the universe is rigged in my favor, channeling one of my favorite poets, Rumi. Maybe, it is the bright, sunny embrace I have on life, and maybe it is just the positive energy I have developed, but it has never failed me. No one wakes up and says they want to make others miserable. So, why approach any relationship with that negative expectation? Life has taught me that everyone is doing the best they can with what they have. If I can show up with a bundle of positivity, skill, and ability to make a positive difference, not be defensive, and look up to others and show them I am willing to take my chances with them, more than 50 percent of the time; people rise up to make that true because it is basic human nature not to want to disappoint. Remember, I said over 50 percent because not every person has the psychological profile to be positive. I need to listen with more than my ears, make my own judgment, and then follow through. This way, I can spot toxic people and avoid contamination. Fifty-fifty chances are better odds than winning the lottery and gambling in Vegas. **I am continuing to learn to take calculated risks with people to build lasting bonds.** Yes, it is a road less traveled in an age where no one trusts anyone else, but my ability to trust and let people in has made my journey a shared joy. As you read this book, you will see how many countless people have enriched my life in so many meaningful ways. **I have also learned to take something positive from every negative experience. Life is a series of lessons, and the more we learn, the richer the tapestry of life gets. In this life, we get back what we put out. Call it Karma or call it basic physics; we create our destiny with our thoughts, words, and actions.**

LESSONS LEARNED:

> *Physical attributes, like the color of skin, texture of hair, body shape, etc., do not define a person* because the person is the embodiment of the soul that dwells within that superficial body.

> *Introspection and self-awareness help develop knowledge* that is vital to building the most important relationship in life, the relationship with oneself, that becomes the foundation for all other relationships in life.

> *None of us should be stereotyped by a single story, and we must strive to burst stereotypes placed upon us.* We must courageously stand up to speak our truth and showcase the composite being that we each are because that will set us free to live our destiny, both as individuals and a human society.

CHAPTER 3

SHAPING THE PATH

"Every moment I shape my destiny with a chisel.
I am the carpenter of my own soul."
—Rumi

Being raised in a Hindu home, living in a Buddhist country, attending a Catholic Convent school run by Holy Family Sisters, and living close to a mosque with calls to prayer five times a day, made for a rather interesting exposure to various religious philosophies as well as practices. A former Portuguese, Dutch, and finally a British colony for almost four hundred years,[5] we had quite a bit of Western influence in our day-to-day lives. **One would not be mistaken in wondering how confusing it could be for a young person when these cultural differences and norms could, at times, send mixed**

messages. For example, we had to wear white uniforms to school, and the uniform had to be exactly knee length. If it was longer, we were expected to hem it since sewing was a craft taught to all girls as part of life skills within the curriculum. On the other hand, if the uniform was short, we were expected to remove the hem and add the missing length. Being a school athlete, representing my age group in national track and field championships, I also wore shorts and t-shirts. Once I got home, I was expected to wear long skirts; no shorts, jeans, or knee-length attire were permitted. In fact, I never wore jeans or trousers until after I was out of my home and living alone.

To help us square all the contradictions, we had a course called Moral Science. In this class, we engaged in active discussions looking at various perspectives of a given issue. No one forced us to think one way or the other, and I felt we were encouraged to voice our thoughts and develop the art of dialogue by listening, evaluating, thoughtfully articulating, and synthesizing to arrive at our own conclusions. My sixth-grade teacher, Rev. Sr. Julia, was also our Moral Science teacher that year. While she was a Catholic nun, she understood us girls so well and had a sense of humor that made her relatable to us. I often wondered what her childhood was like and if she was one of those tomboys like me who had so much spunk and spirit. We never were able to find that out for certain because she had a way of deflating questions about her and making everything about us.

Sr. Julia cared about our psychological development, spiritual core, and physical wellbeing. A keen observer of all her students, she had sage advice for each of us. In my strict traditional Hindu household, my parents overtly lectured us on *how enjoyment was for the westerners, and we should not indulge ourselves,* and *the importance of understanding the difference between acquaintances, colleagues, and friends, so no one crossed the boundaries set in each of those relationships.* We were also segregated by gender, where the girls were not allowed to mingle with the boys. Having two brothers, we always had boys around us, but I had to make tea and call for one of my brothers to come to serve it to their friends, as we girls could not talk to the boys at home. This always felt rather weird because we knew that girls grew up and got married to boys. How do you marry a gender you could not talk to? Moral Science class was where I had the opportunity to ask Sr. Julia all my questions and engage in a human conversation about gender and relationships.

Through my conversations and my writings, Sr. Julia got to know me well. There was a philosophical bend to my writing, even as a child, as a result of my avid reading. After all, how can you talk in a home that discouraged girls from speaking? For a community that worshipped goddesses and presented to the world the first female elected head of state in the 1960s,[6] **I was perpetually puzzled at the mixed messaging.** One evening, my dad sat both my sister and me down to firmly instill in us the importance of being good Hindu girls. Apparently, that included being quiet. His exact words were, "You girls should only speak when spoken to." Utterly confused by this serious edict issued by dad, in the context of us being allowed to talk and play only with girls, my sister had a completely valid question: "If all of us can only speak when spoken to, who gets to speak first?" I was so tickled that she asked the question that I burst out laughing, which did not help matters at all. My poor dad had lost the opportunity to instill a valuable lesson, and we were off laughing and talking, letting him know that his advice made absolutely no sense at all. Poor frustrated Dad just walked away, having given up on both of us.

My parents had us kids after forty and by then had become rather serious in their nature. Having had an arranged marriage, they had to learn about each other following their wedding. Mom was a highly educated university professor, while Dad was an athlete who became a banker without pursuing higher education. Mom was cerebral, while Dad was physical. They had little in common. As a non-demonstrative culture, hugs, kisses, and "I love you" were not things we were ever exposed to. Naturally a sensitive and caring child, I struggled with not having a place to channel my emotions. I excelled in studies, sports, debate, writing, classical dancing, and play-ing the violin because all these got me out of the home and allowed me to be around other children. Sports gave me the opportunity to mingle with students from the Sinhala class; it also gave me the opportunity to have normal relationships with boys. We trained at St. Peter's College track and field, and as their sister school, we often supported each other during athletic competitions.

At times, I wondered if some of my classmates disliked me because I took prizes home for all these activities and was the "**Best All Round Student of the Year**" every year I was at Holy Family Convent, without leaving much on the table for anyone else. **To me, it was not the competition, but the need to put my heart and soul into everything I did. Nothing I accomplished made my parents proud.** In fact, most of the time, they never showed up for my awards nights, never took photographs of my activities, or celebrated my success. My role in life was to learn to cook, clean, and run a household so I could care for my family. The only place I got to be a child was when I was away from home. My parents did not think of it as mean or unreasonable; they were just focused on raising me right as a Hindu girl.

Sr. Julia was putting all the puzzle pieces together and figuring when to broach a conversation with me and how to guide me. One afternoon, the opportunity presented itself. Upon reading my class essay, "Autobiography of an Umbrella," first, she read my submission aloud to the whole class. It was an emotive piece, where my umbrella had been with me as my life companion, and the umbrella's autobiography depicted my story as seen through its eyes. The autobiography of the umbrella started with being a special gift to a little girl to be a companion in life and to protect her from the harsh tropical sun and the tropical monsoons she had to navigate as she lived her life as a schoolgirl.

As her companion, the umbrella got to witness her joys and sorrows and experience her fears and successes. The umbrella witnessed the police stopping the little girl and checking the ID and then subjecting her to cruel treatment because of her race. The umbrella witnessed cars on the road burning with people in it solely because these were Tamil families in a nation where politicians wanted the minority wiped out. It also witnessed the joys of walking along the beach after school, eating peanuts and singing. The umbrella saw how there could be joy and inspiration even amongst death and debris. The umbrella observed how riches could be destroyed, and millionaires can become paupers in a refugee camp in the blink of an eye. It also comprehended that kindness is life-affirming and can transcend all hate to build bridges. Love comes from kindness, compassion, and understanding. It got a life lesson of, "There but for the grace of God, go I." That Tamil essay contained my natural bend toward philosophy and humor, as well as painting a picture of a child struggling to find her place in this world. A world that was hard, cruel, yet beautiful and kind. That was the first time I saw Sr. Julia cry, and through her tears, she finished reading my essay for the class.

Once the class was over, Sr. Julia asked me to stay back so she could talk to me. I was not sure what to expect, but I knew she would not hurt my feelings; that was not her style. She asked me to sit next to her, and we talked. We spoke like two adults; I was mature beyond my age. **I will never forget her priceless message to me.**

Kasthuri, you have the gift of kindness and compassion. Treat this as a gift given to you by God. While this is the most precious of all gifts, this gift will also be your cross to bear. Promise me that you will not throw away this gift, but learn how to use it to enrich those around you while preserving yourself. Child, remember that anything that harms your spirit will debilitate your soul and become toxic to your body. It will help you find that balance but learn to lead with that soul God has blessed you with. Kindness and caring will be viewed as weakness by cruel and controlling people. You are a strong girl with a will of steel and gift of gab. God would not have given you such a wonderful gift that is also a burden if he did not believe you would have the strength to handle it.

We both cried, hugged each other, and talked for a while about the challenges I would face growing up.

The following week, during the Moral Science class, Sr. Julia brought up kindness, caring, and loving. She wanted us girls to understand that these were noble qualities; qualities Jesus Christ embodied. We talked about how being a Christian is about embodying the message of Christ, which is no different from the message of all the religions we were learning about in school. Without ending the discussion there, she took it one step further by talking to us about how parents will try to guilt us into doing what they want for us in life. **She wanted each of us to shape our path and live our truth without compromising our authenticity. To her, we were all her girls. Our happiness was her joy. Our peace was her goal.**

"Your parents may use emotional blackmail to force you to do things you do not want to do. Take it from me: no one dies until it is their time to go. You and your actions will never be the cause of their death. Choose what works for you. When you are grown up, and you find yourself in a place without support to follow your heart, come find me. I will support you. Live and experience love. Don't be afraid to care, share, and embrace joy."

We were growing up fast, thrust into the beauty and ugliness around us concurrently, where it was easy to lose ourselves and forget each of our unique gifts given to us at birth by our maker. It was her mission to help us realize our God-given potential. We all loved her for it. We all still visit her from time to time, as each of us returns home. Sr. Julia gave me a part of her in sixth grade. It is the part that sits on my right shoulder, motivating me to lead with my soul. It is the part of me that has learned to value kindness and compassion alongside strategy and success. She taught me that I was enough because God would not have made me and given me life if I were not ready. She helped me understand that it is perfectly fine to be caring and kind while being firm and assertive. Being no-nonsense and loving or being firm and kind are not incompatible. Listening with my heart, smiling with my eyes, and feeling with my soul are all priceless gifts given to me so I could pass them on to fellow travelers.

I was the child whose life goal was to be happy. Not become a doctor, engineer, professor, or CFO. To me, those were things I could do but who I was to become was to be the embodiment of my soul. I wanted to become happy and peaceful. **Becoming a CFO in my early thirties for a Fortune-500 company was neither a goal nor an ambition I actively pursued, but the skills and circumstances presented themselves to put me there. I continue to be an enigma to my fellow executives and finance professionals.** I am often told, "You are too kind to be a finance executive," or asked, "How can you be successful as a finance leader by being nice to everyone?" Let's take a moment and break down the question. Aren't we all human beings first? Is there not a difference between who a person is and what they do for a living? My response is **always, "I am a human being who happens to have chosen the field of finance; I am not a finance professional who happens to be human."** Forcing folks to ponder the meaning of what I had just said, "Reading Shakespeare when growing up in Sri Lanka, I learned from Hamlet that how I treat people is a reflection of my station in life and how you do is a reflection of yours. I am at total peace at the station I am at, but are you?"

When it came to select my doctoral dissertation topic, I chose moral cognitive capability of a CFO team and how it impacts the sustained value creation goal of a corporation.[7] **I developed an ethical leadership model that is rooted in noble character traits that lay the foundation for effective leadership, influencing employees of an organization to drive market goals of brand loyalty and innovation, central**

for delivering the business goals of sustainable long-term value creation and brand value. One of the two people I dedicated my dissertation to was Sr. Julia, for she was the one who paved the way for the young girl to grow up without compromising her courage of conviction. Because of her presence in my life, I have learned to cherish the part of me that dares to be kind and cares enough to show compassion. Because of her, I live an authentic life without apologizing for leading with my soul. She helped me build on the foundation Thevar had helped lay down.

A large part of my professional success is owed to Sr. Julia and her guidance. I did not become a young CFO because of what I did. I got there because of who I had become. A leader capable of inspiring others and holding space for them to fearlessly innovate and thrive so the organization could grow. My education, technical skills, communication, etc., definitely helped; do not for a minute think they did not have a role, but it was who I was that helped me influence results by enabling and ennobling others. I am acutely aware of the fact that who I am shapes what I do and how I do it. Just as rising tides raise all boats, I focused on lifting others, not because I was vying for sainthood, but because that is what gives me peace and joy; career success followed.

We each shape our path by charting our destiny. Life is not a spectator sport; it requires active engagement. In the end, it is not about all the things done to us, but about how we act on the face of those challenges and who we become at the core of our being. It is always about our respective souls, and the character chiseled into our soul. Where one person sees a rock, an artist sees a hidden sculpture to be brought to life. We each have the ability to determine who we become. The journey of self-discovery is a life-long one, and when done right, it never ceases to be amazing. It is, after all, human to seek happiness, and how could we each seek our own happiness if we never made the time to understand what happiness means to us individually? Life must be more than a series of jobs, titles, and work. It ought to hold a deeper meaning to the soul as we build ourselves piece by piece.

LESSONS LEARNED:

➢ **Have the courage to be kind and approach work as well as life with empathy, knowing it is not a weakness; it is a relationship-building superpower** *that holds space for others while helping you evolve as an influential leader.*

➢ **Kindness, compassion, and empathy are not incongruent with success**; *they are the seedlings from which success grows because nothing in life is accomplished in a vacuum in the absence of fellow travelers enabling and ennobling that success.*

➢ **The pursuit of happiness is a common thread that unites us all**. *If we develop the awareness and ability to see that and engage with fellow travelers to seek understanding, we can succeed and thrive.*

CHAPTER 4

TEACHING TO LEARN

*"If you light a lamp for someone else,
it will also brighten your path."*
—Buddha

Our formal education was mother-tongue based. Upon independence from the British empire, the newly formed Sri Lankan government eliminated English education and replaced it with Sinhala and Tamil language-based education, preparing students for the GCE O/L and A/L, the British public exam model. Regardless of the intent, the result was a racially segregated society where children were placed in different classrooms for learning and interacting with those from the same race. My parents' generation was educated and were functional in English, having been raised under the

British Rule while we kids had to learn in Tamil. At Holy Family Convent, we had four Sinhala classes and one Tamil class for each grade to reflect the racial breakdown of the community proportionately. This also meant that our parents could not help us with schoolwork, given their proficiency in Tamil across the various subject matters was not up to par. Anyone who grew up learning in another language knows the counting and thinking always remain in the functional language, regardless of the development of additional language skills. I still count in Tamil and know my tables in Tamil, even though I have been working in the Western business world for more than twenty-five years.

My teachers had a creative way to solve this dilemma of the lack of parental support for learning. They paired up students who were doing well in the class with students who were struggling and had us teach and tutor our classmates. Looking back, I think this was ingenious of them. Students who were ahead of the class did not get bored and cause mischief; students who were lagging did not get left behind. **We were responsible for our collective success, and our creativity in teaching our peers was totally unbridled.** I always had two of my classmates on either side of me during class so I can help them along. I would have to continually find creative ways to explain concepts to my peer study team, which kept me attuned to how they each learn and what captures their imagination. My creative approach to teaching at the post-secondary level for twenty years can be directly attributed to this single methodology of *learning by teaching peers*. Teaching without any semblance of authority but sheer creativity to engage others was a skill that has come in handy beyond the educator role and spilled into my practitioner role where I am able to take my colleagues along for a journey of continuous improvement as a financial agent for change in the international business arena.

Both my study buddies did not come from Tamil-speaking homes but had to choose between Tamil or Sinhala. One was from a Catholic family that spoke mostly English at home while the other was Muslim and did not have Tamil as her native tongue. Learning to be sensitive to each of their family norms was important for me because I sincerely cared about all three of us doing well in school. Therefore, I visited their homes regularly, getting to know their families, and teaching them in their home environment. We bonded over the years, learning and growing up together. We celebrated each other's holidays, enjoyed each other's cultures, and embraced one another wholeheartedly, only as children would. Hanging out with them gave me the opportunity to practice my English and develop my third language in addition to taking Elocution lessons to speak it as if it was my native language.

One of the girls sang like an angel and loved to bake. Baking being a western form of cooking, it was the Catholics on the island who excelled in baking and decorating cakes. This girl knew her baking, and I was beginning to learn the art of baking by merely observing her. I began to realize that baking was chemistry, and there was plenty of science involved in the process. Which meant, when I am helping my friend learn science-related subjects I could draw from baking. We had arithmetic, algebra, geometry, trigonometry, and mental math as separate course work alongside physics, chemistry, biology, health science, and home science. Equally important were religious studies, arts and crafts, music, dancing, languages with literature, social studies, and moral science. Looking back, we certainly had a rich curriculum helping us prepare for life.

As we were preparing for our final exam, I wanted to make sure my friend fully understood the function of skin and what the cross-section of the skin looked like when illustrated. I figured, if she remembered how to draw the cross-section and label all the parts, then she could apply that knowledge to answer any questions on the exam. The trick, however, was in demonstrating it in an ideal manner for her to remember. Like most evenings, I had walked over to this girl's home where her parents welcomed me with cheer, and her mom, whom I always called "Aunty," served me some of her delicious cake and tea. As I was enjoying teatime with my friend, a bright idea appeared. After tea, I asked Aunty if my friend and I could study in the kitchen, and we were given the green light.

Once in the kitchen, I had my friend get out her rectangular baking tray, long wooden spoon, and all the different utensils and decorating implements. My friend frowned at me, asking what I was trying to do. I asked her to be patient with me while I opened the health science book to the page containing the cross-section of the skin. We decided to play a game by replicating the diagram on the kitchen table using all her baking and decorating implements. The rectangular baking tray formed the cross-section of the skin, the wooden ladle with its oval spoon and long tapering handle became the hair follicle, and so on until we had the diagram replicated. It was an evening filled with girlish giggles, amazement at how kitchen tools doubled up as practical learning tools, and pride in turning learning into fun-filled play.

Next week for our final exam, we certainly had that question on human skin. We looked up at each other and exchanged that knowing smile, signaling to each other that we got this one. Needless to say, she did well on the exam, making us both happy. The teacher was quite curious as to how we mastered this and other diagrams of human anatomy so well. **When we shared our kitchen table creativity approach to human anatomy, she encouraged our out-of-the-box thinking and cheered us on to continue making learning fun.**

My other friend was the life of the class. Her vivid imagination and storytelling were legendary. If we were not prepared to take a test in class, she would faint on cue, causing pandemonium in class, necessitating two to three of us girls to carry her to the sick room. We had this biology teacher who was rather inconsiderate in the way she spoke to the students, and my friend decided she had enough for the day. Partway through class, this girl started goofing off, and the teacher started name-calling her and referring to her as crazy. That was the opening my other friend needed. She packed up her book bag and walked right out of class. The teacher stopped her as she was getting out the door and asked where she thought she was going, and this girl replied, "To the nuthouse, of course; where else?" and kept walking. That was the end of that day's biology class because the teacher completely and utterly lost it.

She was a creative and mischievous classmate who was different from the rest of the students because she was the only Muslim girl. Some teachers did not understand that her frame of reference was rather different from the rest of the students. I had always felt that she used her outlandish stories and mischievous behavior as a way to mask her language difficulty and cultural difference in an effort to fit in. I saw a kind and caring young girl, who was my friend. What stands out to me most about this girl, in addition to all the laughs she gave me, was her deep sense of caring.

Sri Lanka was in the middle of a thirty-year civil war while we were growing up, and the Tamil people were the ethnic minority persecuted by the Sinhala government. Every four years, when we had our national elections, one of the two Sinhala parties, United National Party (UNP) or Sri Lankan Freedom Party (SLFP), came into power. Tamils were the swing vote, and the losing party would attack Tamil homes, burn homes, kill families, rape mothers and daughters in front of fathers and sons, and commit other inhumane acts while the government sat in silence and the rest of the world carried on with blinders. My dad's bank would place a security guard at our home, and the nuns took us kids into the convent for our safety every four years. My mom, being a teacher at St. Bridget's Convent, spent time at the nunnery and visited with the nuns in the infirmary during the weeks leading up to and following each election. Despite this protection, we still witnessed and survived horrible things that were part of the war. These things shaped my perspective and outlook on life and created a desire and need to look at things in a positive way. There can be so much in life we can't control that can happen to us. But I have discovered we can choose our response to it. We can choose gratitude, kindness, and unity.

Having a Catholic friend who had quite a bit of western influence and a Muslim friend who was excluded from racial profiling was helpful in learning survival skills by adopting culturally diverse behaviors. The European decedents on the island were called Berger. **Nuns had asked all of Tamil Hindu girls to stop wearing cultural symbols for our own safety.** We all wore a black dot on our forehead, called "Pottu," and that was the first identifier that gave us away when our school bus was stopped, and the girls were checked for our ethnicity. At home, the message was that I needed to be a good traditional Hindu girl respectful of the culture. I knew I had to take matters into my own hands to make sure I survived and thrived in spite of what was going on inside the home and outside in society. **As a young Tamil girl, my priorities were certainly different from the adults; it was survival. Surviving all cruelty only humans can dish out to other humans and getting out of the country the first opportunity I got.** My two friends and their families were helping me in countless ways that even I had not realized at that time. I was learning the art of cultural diversity and the art of blending in and transforming to survive.

As soon as I finished my GCE O/L, tenth grade, I decided to pursue my high school in India. India was close enough to come home if the need arose but got me out of the civil war, of which I wanted no part. It was only increasing fear, hate, and animosity within the communities on the island, and I saw no good coming out of such inhumane actions that were continuously escalating. I shared the news in school and was packing up to leave. The evening before my departure, I had a surprising visitor. My Muslim friend arrived after dusk in an auto-rickshaw with a parting gift for me. I was pleasantly surprised that she had come, given the prevailing condition on the island, so late and bearing a gift. That night, this childhood friend had given me a gift that will keep on giving for the rest of my life.

It was a simple gift, a word of hope, given by one young girl to another. There was deep wisdom in it. What I had received was a glass-framed quote with a picture. Two little kittens were hanging upside down on the handle of a flower basket, unsure of how to land right-side-up without getting hurt, accompanied by the words, **"Faith isn't faith until it is ALL you are holding on to." She had just given me the gift I needed, a gift to remind me of the unwavering faith that we will each land on our own two feet, somehow, someday, someplace. We were going to be okay.** That evening, I needed that more than anything else.

The glass broke over the years, but the words and the message continue to live on in my heart and will follow me till I take my last breath because without faith, there is no hope, and without hope, there is no tomorrow. **While I was teaching my friends the course work, we were learning basic humanity from each other. We were learning to love and let go, with faith that we will meet again.** We were learning to defy the adult world filled with anger, envy, and hate to build our own bridges of hope and faith.

My foundational education and the way we were allowed to learn is something I will never trade for all the gold in the world. Yes, we had to deal with violence in a war-torn island nation, but that too was part of our education. Adapting to different situations, having the ability to learn from situations and people around me, keeping the faith, and staying the course to see through what I started are all skills that have proven to be ageless. Today, as a global mergers and acquisition finance professional with expertise in post-acquisition operational integration to unleash the deal value, I had to learn the pre-acquisition and post-acquisition organizational environments, the value proposition, and how to shape the change by influencing a global team without having direct authority over them. Being an organizational change agent in a dynamic global economy is akin to riding an elephant.[8] Unlike a horse that could be directed by the rider, the elephant cannot be. One must influence the elephant, so the elephant chooses to head toward the intended strategic direction. **Organizational inertia is akin to an elephant.** If the rider comes across as forcing the elephant, the elephant will find a way to unmount the rider by force and destroy the rider, just like organizational inertia would a person working against the collective will.

One of the reasons I continue to teach is to keep my mind sharp and creative juices flowing. I grew up teaching as a means of learning. Learning is not about knowing facts. It is about understanding, applying, driving agile decisions, and influencing change. As a faculty member of Southern Illinois University Chicago Programs, I teach public safety and homeland security administration for fire, police, and homeland security professionals as well as electronics technology management and project management for the US military. My students of twenty years are mostly men in their forties and fifties from these professions, making public safety, homeland security, and military decisions applying data analytics, economics, public policy, finance, and strategic leadership in solving real-world problems. When I am at North Park University in Chicago, I am teaching both business and non-profit professionals in the MBA program to help make real-world decisions in global organizational settings. I am able to take my practitioner world examples and experiences into my classroom, apply them to solving my student's challenges, then take the lessons learned from the classroom creative problem-solving back into the workplace to enrich my business life. Teaching and learning both help me be in tune with human behavior as well as remain agile in influencing an organization to realize its strategic growth. These are skills rooted in my early introduction to teaching and learning with my classmates. While we all grew up to be different individuals over the years, the opportunity provided to me at Holy Family Convent to expand the boundaries of how things are done to hone my unique approach has remained a foundational pillar. It is amazing how a country and culture that contains an underpinning of collective social contract developed its young to embrace individuality without calling it as such, thus teaching us the importance of balancing the two.

Individualism for self-development and collectivism for societal sustainability can co-exist. Shared prosperity is possible. I live in the US today, surrounded by the notion that winning is everything, and if you are not a winner, you are a loser. This is not real, and this is not sustainable. What is winning? Is it to have more money and material than the others? If that happened, can I eat that money? Can I live in it? Can I wear it? Can it heal my heart? I chose to pursue a different definition of winning. It is a winning where everyone can benefit. If I shared my knowledge instead of hoarding it at work, the organization becomes sustainable, and business continuity can take place. If I shared my earnings by way of sharing meals with others, I get to build relationships that are nurturing. If I help strangers in a meaningful way, I shape the community I live in to make my life more fulfilling.

In each of the scenarios noted, everyone wins. Any relationship that is predicated on one person gaining and another losing is not sustainable because what is the incentive for those who do not gain to participate or be engaged? Why would anyone invest time, energy, and commitment for no return on that investment? In that case, "He who does least does most," the Zen philosophy comes true. I hold the belief that "If you are not a winner, you are a loser" is a false dichotomy that can be harmful. Win-win partnerships are sustainable, and rewarding was a lesson I have imprinted as I continue to chisel my destiny.

One could authentically grow up to who they were meant to be and never forget that they are part of a larger community with a duty toward each other. This is what I love about my native country. **Despite all the ugliness of the war perpetrated by the politicians, civilians sincerely cared about one another and looked out for each other.** There definitely was beauty and joy once you got past the horrors of civil war, and that too was a lesson worth learning in childhood. After all, rainbows are found only around a storm, are they not? How could we ever learn to appreciate the silver lining if we never saw a dark thunder cloud?

LESSONS LEARNED:

➢ **Knowledge is power, and that power comes not by hoarding but by sharing, exploring, and continuously creating new ways to seek it.**

➢ **A mindful, responsible leader knows that individualism to strive for personal improvement and collectivism to build collaborative teams are both equally vital for success.** True leadership lies in balancing the two instead of pontificating on false dichotomies of forcing others to choose one over the other.

➢ **Challenges come our way to strengthen us and polish our souls to seek greatness.** Giving into struggles is not what the human journey is about. It is about building resiliency to use the roadblocks as stepping-stones and see the silver lining in each cloud. Success is forged by continuous polishing and never giving up on ourselves and others around us.

CHAPTER 5

PERSPECTIVE IS EVERYTHING

"You are not a drop in the ocean.
You are the entire ocean in a drop."
—Rumi

On the fateful day of July 1983, I was all ready to go to school, excited about mid-year report cards in eighth grade. The fisherman who occupies our street corner at the intersection of the main road came running, pleading with my father not to send the children to school, insisting the whole family stay home. He advised us to have a "go bag" ready, just in case because things might take a bad turn. There was talk about a major attack on the Tamil families by the government. Dad insisted that he had to be at the bank but gave orders to us to stay home and stay safe.

Mom was not someone who could handle such stress. Her coping mechanism was to cry and speak her woes in a loud voice. My younger brother and I were the bold ones, and we spoke Sinhala fluently. A young lady down our street had been tutoring us so we could all talk our way out of situations by not coming across as Tamil children. Our neighbor was a beautiful Sinhala lady married to a Tamil man. She had asked us to tell the military or anyone who storms into our home that she is our aunt. This would give her the opportunity to protect us without being harmed herself. We kept all the doors and windows open to prevent a break-in. We set up chairs in the backyard to lift Mom and push her over the property wall into the neighbor's yard if our home was attacked. Mom, as a heart patient, could not run, climb, or jump.

My kid brother, who was just one year younger than me, had an uncanny sense of humor with the ability to talk utter rubbish and make light of any situation, just like me. It was a survival tactic we both had developed, aided by the middle-child syndrome. Mom saw nothing good in how we approached life-or-death situations. She did not see the power in going out with a laugh, not giving into fear. We both knew that we were the family clowns who leveraged the clowning as a strategy for distraction and survival. We both practiced our plan by pushing mom over the wall a couple of times. We were kids, and she was a bit heavy. I am sure we bruised her and made her feel like we were throwing her over the wall. She started crying and told us that we were going to kill her long before we were attacked. So, we stopped practicing and got her commitment not to scream or cry. Brother was on the roof, keeping an eye on what was going on; he was our lookout. I was inside the home with Mom and the remaining two siblings. We gathered yard and kitchen implements we could use as weapons when we were attacked.

It evolved into a slow-moving day of updates on what was going on, street by street, as the Tamil homes and businesses came under attack. All residential streets are off the main highway, Galle Road, with businesses lining both sides of Galle

Road. Our street was right across from the local police station. In most countries, that should make our street safe. However, in an age of ethnic cleansing, the proximity meant our risk as the persecuted minority increased. We could see the fire and smoke filling up the air. Store owners and workers were badly beat-up and came running down the street bleeding. Everyone pitched in to provide whatever crude approaches at our disposal to help stop the bleeding and prevent deaths, all the while ready to be attacked ourselves. **I do not recall anyone crying or arguing. There was the eerie resignation that we just do what we can for as long as we can. Neighbors were ready to help neighbors. It did not matter who was a stranger and who was a neighbor. At that moment, we were all human, and we were going to do everything in our power to save lives. Property was not a consideration. Lives were what mattered.**

It was not the age of smartphones, and the government had shut off the power. As dusk settled in, we knew the business destructions were over, and harming families and homes had begun. **Tamils, Sinhalese, Muslims, and Bergers all lived side by side in this urban city. That was going to be our strength. When one home burned, all homes would be impacted. We inherently understood our mutual dependency, and the non-Tamil neighbors had a plan to protect as many lives as possible.** Agreements were made that women and children will be moved into unharmed non-Tamil homes while the men took the roof. We were going to share whatever food was available, and we were going to protect lives the best we can, knowing we were facing the government forces.

Dad was not home yet. We had no way of reaching him or knowing if he was alive. We placed our makeshift weapons on either side of the entry door and in strategic places with the goal of protecting Mom because we could not let the attackers harm her in any way. These men exerted power by raping mothers and daughters in front of their sons and fathers. We knew it. We had to fight with all we had if it came to that. Not having electricity only exacerbated the stressful situation.

Flashlights were our only guide because candles were a risk, given that burning our home would be one of the goals of our attackers, and we were not going to give them a head start on flames in the home. I remember sitting in the dark, gripping a yard implement, English name of it escapes me to this day, wondering, *why do men demonstrate their power by demeaning and dehumanizing mothers and daughters? What is about being a man gave them that callous arrogance that dignity and protection of a woman were not a consideration?* It occurred to me at that moment, when we get raided, I needed to make sure they do not see me as a girl, but a child. My survival depended on our attackers not seeing Mom or my baby sister and seeing me as just a child, a child in one of their families. **My little brother and I were going to find a way to talk our way out of this, and we were going to do it using their language.** Yard implements were our backup plan.

In a child's mind, it seemed like a good plan. Then, there was a bang on the front door, and it was being pushed open. We stood on either side of the opening door, ready to execute our plan. If we could talk our way out of this and we would know that in the first few seconds. Then we would know if we should use the implements. We also agreed that we are not going without a fight. We were going to die, and we were going out blazing! To our surprise and utter horror, it was Dad. We were happy we did not attack first! He explained that he had to walk along the beach to get home because the highway was blazing as businesses were on fire—what a relief. At least the family was together; Dad was alive.

Neighboring streets were under attack, and we were taking in families into non-Tamil homes down our street. **Age and race did not matter that night. We all did what we could to keep each other safe, calm, and protected. The best of everyone showed up at a time of pure madness. This gave me hope for us and who we are as people. We were Sri Lankans that night. Each one was their brother's and sister's keeper.** Street by street, the destruction continued for days. August 3 came around, and my little brother was sad his birthday was going to be remembered for hate and killing. Not having a cake is one thing, but not knowing if we would live is a whole other ball game. Close to the police station was a bakery owned by a Sinhala family, and our neighbors knew the bakery would be in-tact. One of the men went to the bakery and brought back a loaf of bread. That was all that was available, and it was not for sale. He had just taken it, determined to show a child his birthday mattered. In the dark, with flashlights, we sang happy birthday to my brother, and we all shared a loaf of bread.

The fishermen at the top of our street protected the street. The neighbors protected our homes. No one knew how long we could keep this up, and the adults decided it was time to get the women and children to safety. In a language-segregated society, my brothers went to a Tamil boys-only school. We not only separated children by language; we also separated them by gender. My sister and I went to a Catholic Convent school, where we had four Sinhala classes and one Tamil class for each grade. While we never sat in the same class to learn, as a school athlete, I trained with the Sinhala class girls. We started hearing that the school my brothers went to was turning into a refugee camp as all the surviving Tamil people started showing up on school property, having no other place to go.

Those few days of sheer mayhem would stay with me forever. I saw how wealth, power, position, and social status did not matter when it came to this life-or-death situation. **Relationships each one had invested in, the humanity with each person lived their life, and how they had touched the lives of others were what counted. This experience affirmed my core belief that my knowledge, my relationship with my God, and how I engage with others are the only three things that can never be taken from me.** Those are a part of my soul. They matter. Watching rich and powerful men sleeping on the floor of a stranger's home covered in blood, consumed with grief, having watched all the women in the family brutalized and killed was a horrendous moment of truth.

I was scared, scared for my own dignity. I was scared for my family. I was beyond angry that our government would do this to us. I was angry that in a democracy, the adults had allowed things to get this far without fighting back. I was angry that we were all losing our childhood for no valid reason but for the twist of fate. I was angry that the hateful attackers were blind to the fact that their own children are watching their friends and neighbors killed as their own childhood disappeared. How can a society of educated adults with a tolerant society embracing all the major religions, ethnicities, and lifestyles descend into this madness? When did Buddhism become the root of such evil and heinous genocide? Why did the rest of the world not care? Fear, anger, and roiling questions kept me going. Surprisingly, all the love and caring around me taught me love and humanity would triumph despite the hate of a few conservative men.

It was decided that Mom and the four children had to leave Colombo for our safety. However, going to Jaffna, the heart and home of the Tamil people, was not safe because we could all be bombed into oblivion. Batticaloa was an east coast city where my dad's brother lived, and it was deemed safer due to the Tamil and Muslim integrated society. A mixed environment was safer for us as Tamils than a segregated Tamil city. The Muslim neighbors and friends brought their clothes and dressed us all up to look like them. They even drove us to the train station and set us off on a one-way journey. We were Tamil refugees. A refugee family, separated from each other, as Dad stayed back in Colombo.

Dad had asked me to make sure I hold the family together as the oldest daughter and keep everyone safe. At age five, I took this responsibility seriously. I was raised to be the mother, given our mom's health condition and the risk of living in a society of ethnic cleansing. Mom married my dad after she was thirty-five years of age and had four children after the age of forty, all fourteen to eighteen months apart. When my little sister was born, she had a heart failure and did not come home with the newborn. I will never forget the day I visited her through a glass window, and a kind neighbor had baked a cake decorated with two cats to cheer me up for my birthday. We had my birthday at the hospital, not knowing if Mom would live through her heart condition. I knew my duty was to be the mother, and I had already been taking on responsibilities. However, this was different. I was going to be alone with Mom and the kids. We were refugees. I had no idea what that meant. I had no idea what awaited us. Yet, I had to be the responsible one. I was scared out of my wits, but hell-bent on not showing it to anyone.

My uncle met us at the Batticaloa station and took us to his home. We had a roof over our heads. Mom and my aunt did not see eye to eye, and the sparks started flying right off the bat. We could not cook in the kitchen. I had to use bricks in the backyard to cook. I did not mind all of that, but I had little patience for the two adult women behaving like mean teen-age girls. Mom still harbored hate and anger that the dowry she brought into her arranged marriage with dad was used to educate his brother, and this couple with no children had been the benefactors of both her money and jewelry. I, on the other hand, did not need this soap opera. Not at this juncture.

My uncle was not at all urban. He was even more conservative than my dad. He had never lived in Colombo and felt that I was too westernized. I was all wrong, and he was not going to make my life easy. My brothers were given bicycles to ride to school. My sister and I had to walk miles, crossing a bridge shared for trains and automobiles to get to school. Girls did not get any consideration, especially westernized independent girls like me.

Stuck amongst the pettiness of the adults, the raging civil war in Colombo, and not knowing how Dad was holding up alone, trying to settle into a conservative community that did not see me as someone who fitted in and trying to navigate a new school was maddening. Walking was a wonderful way to calm me down. I talked a lot to myself. I trusted no one. I had lost all respect for adults. I knew I was on my own, and **I had**

to make sure the five of us survived the next six months so my older brother could finish tenth grade before our parents can safely get him out of the country. This was all being done to assure his education and survival. He was going to carry the family name, and he had to be protected. I had a mission: Get the hell out of this place with the family intact. It could be worse. We could be in a refugee camp with diseases spreading and exposed to bombing. I had to learn to mask my anger. I had to become a sweet-talking actress to get my way and stay safe. I did just that. I became a student of human behavior. I learned by observing and figured out where I can make inroads. I planned to win over one person at a time.

An all-girls Tamil only school with 100 percent conservative girls who thought I was an entitled westernized urban princess was difficult to swallow. They talked about me right in front of me based on the assumption that I was not fluent in Tamil. I was slow to make friends because I was not ready to open myself up to anything. Life was a mess already, and I did not need eighth-grade drama. I did not feel like a child. I could not relate to these girls. They had no clue what we had just survived. They hated me being there. **I was the outsider who did not belong. Ironic for a Tamil girl to find out that I did not belong with my people because of their prejudice of the urban society I came from. I was not Tamil enough for them. I was not Hindu enough for them. I had found more love, acceptance, and humanity in Colombo amidst the civil war.** My own people, young girls, were being utterly nasty toward me. I carried Sr. Julia on my shoulder and kept reminding myself not to let any of this get to me. I could not let anything around me break my spirit.

As we completed assignments and teachers started giving out grades, my new classmates were in for a big surprise. I was an excellent writer in both Tamil and English. My writing had the power to evoke emotions. My new teachers were touched by my prose, not just the words but the messages contained within. I was good at math and science as well. I was at the top of my class in Colombo, and these girls in Batticaloa were starting to realize that I was going to top the class. A refugee girl is going to be the first, and they had underestimated my language proficiency. I remained my approachable, kind, and caring self but never trusted anyone and never let anyone in. I had a fortress built around me. Six months would fly by, and I would be back in Colombo to pick up the pieces and to move on with life, whatever that meant.

Military checkpoints, snipers shooting, and ultra-conservatism surrounded me. **Men in this conservative community thought a so-called westernized girl was open season. I did not feel safe walking to school and back with the nasty things said to me.** I even started walking in the middle of the road to avoid crude men on the sidewalks. My little sister, oblivious to all this, assumed that I was being difficult. I decided enlightening her might further take away her childhood. One of us losing it is bad enough; I had to let her keep some semblance of it. One day, the neighborhood bull decided to chase me down the road and knock me with his horn. Luckily, I got away with just my book bag getting tossed. The family laughed about how Kasthuri picked a fight with the bull, and I let them have their fun. Trying to explain to them the horrors of being demeaned and sexualized by random men on the street was not a conversation I wanted to have with my family. Especially the family that believed I was dark-skinned and, therefore, ugly. I know from experience they would tell me that I was making things up to get attention because I had my beautiful sister beside me. They would tell me I was jealous and remind me that no man would ever want to marry me. To this day, I have just let it go. That was not the mountain I was going to die on. I had a life to live. Everyone is entitled to their perspective. I just had to live my truth in a meaningful way to myself. I had nothing to prove to anyone.

Finally, this nightmare came to an end, and we returned to Colombo. My older brother was sent to India with a host family established to guide him through high school. Dad was transferred to the Middle East for work. I was in our home in Colombo with mom and the two younger siblings. While life in Colombo never felt the same again, I was happy to be back. I had neighbors and friends who understood me. This was an urban society with which I had a sense of belonging. Going back to my convent school was heartbreaking because not all the girls came back. We did not know which of the ones who did not return lived and which ones died. We could not find them. We had all lost a piece of us. My close friend's home was burned, and I heard her family had become refugees. She and I were athletes and spent all our free time training together. To lose my friend, like that, with no goodbyes, could not be put into words. **My walls stayed up. I have always been a guarded child. Everyone saw me as a good student, athlete, talented in the arts, kind, happy, and helpful. No one saw the inner struggles, hurt, anger, and fear.** Only Sr. Julia had some idea, but I had mastered the art of not being read. It was about self-preservation at home and in society. I needed to be aware and able to read others but can never let my guard down.

I started hearing my parents talking on the phone about getting me married so I can be taken care of by the man who marries me and possibly leave the country. I was seeing this happen to other Tamil girls, where parents arranged dowry marriages for their daughters and sent them off to another country with a husband she did not know, into a life she had no clue as to what awaited her. Aunties in the neighborhood started telling me what I needed to do and how I should behave to have a potential groom want to marry me. **If there was anger inside me, all this was making me livid! My mind was made up. I was never going to get married. I did not need a man to take care of me. I was going to make it on my own. I had a plan for it.**

One weekend, I took the sewing scissors and cut my long hair. My natural waves made me look like a rock star, and my mom was scandalized. She cried for days. All the aunties were brought in for an intervention. I was asked what could be done if the prospective groom preferred long hair? "I have no objection to him growing his own hair long," was my curt response. That did not help the situation, but they all stormed off after yelling at me.

I completed the tenth grade and was exploring my exit plan while awaiting the public exam results. With Dad away, my mom felt she had lost total control over me as I was not heeding her advice of being a conservative Hindu girl. Because I was not light-skinned, marriage proposals that came preferred to wait for my sister for a couple of years. Mom was growing frustrated by the day. I did not let any of this bother me because I now had just over fifteen years of conditioning of being told why I was all wrong, and God was punishing Mom for her bad karma by having me born as her oldest daughter. My oldest fair-skinned brother should have been the daughter, and I should have been the son, according to Mom. My mom wanted two light-skinned daughters, and I had spoiled her plans. Mom also insisted that the fair-skinned kids played together, and they were to grow up as friends while the two dark-skinned middle children were to stay in their lane. It was deeply hurtful, but there was nothing I could do. I knew I had my wit and my abilities that would set me free. I had a caring personality that would open doors for me.

Mom also believed that preparing me for an arranged marriage included breaking me like I was a wild horse. She had talked my younger brother into "breaking me." Most children want to please their parents and earn their love. I understand why my brother willingly did what she asked him to do. I had zero desire to please Mom because that meant I lose myself to gain her approval. **I did not believe in losing my soul in pursuit of anything. Not love. Not acceptance. Not approval. Not success.** Naturally, a physical altercation broke when my younger brother punched my nose and broke it. I was not going to take it without a fight. I was an athlete. I ran long distance and had the stamina for endurance. I was also a discus and shot-put thrower. That is where I channeled my anger. I represented my school and won national trophies because my anger fueled me. I channeled my anger at the situation into my strength and endurance to lambast my brother. He was taught, in the past, never to touch me. He broke the cardinal rule. He was going to learn a lesson. I had a broken nose, but he had his share of damage.

True to form, Mom had all the same aunties around yelling at me for not being a girl and acting like a boy. Apparently, I had failed to accept my karma as a girl and take the beating. None of these grown women saw violence against a girl as an offense. Violence against girls, sponsored by the mothers to control the daughters, was a common practice and, in my eyes, grooming the sons to grow up to be abusers. I feared that my brother might grow up believing he could physically abuse his future wife and daughters because that was how his mom was raising him. It was not just the civil war; the traditional homes were also a problem. I realized that conservatism, be it Buddhist, Hindu, Christian, or any other, had their roots in control, bias, and violence. **I was going to find a way out of all this. I wrote to my dad, who was in Oman at that time. I told him that I am leaving home with or without his permission. If he had any interest in continuing to have me as his daughter, he could help me get out. If I left on my own, I was never coming back.**

To my surprise, Dad made arrangements with his bank colleagues to help me move to India. Mom was upset, but she had no say in the matter. I had learned to make my own clothes by then, and I had a new wardrobe made for my trip, including a three-piece skirt suit for my flight. It was my flight of freedom, and I was going to exit like the rock star everyone thought I was because of my hair. I took great joy in designing and sewing my clothes. It was a way for me to accept my body and my looks, growing up in a home that denied me that acceptance.

All this was going on within the framework of the continued civil war. By now, the Tamil youth had organized and were mounting a fight against the Sinhala government. Liberation Tigers of Tamil Eelam (LTTE) was the separatist movement that was demanding the Tamil autonomy as an opposition to the ethnic cleansing so the Tamil people can retain their homeland. This resulted in the ongoing bombing on the island. Midnight raids of Tamil homes took place in Colombo to see if we were harboring LTTE members. Checking school buses and mandatory profiling of all Tamil people was commonplace. Every day we went out to school or anywhere else, we did not know if we would come home alive. It is hard to imagine; amidst all this, my family had taken the course it had.

When we got raided, I would talk to the young soldiers, offer them tea, and speak to them in their language. Life had taught me, if I create a moment of respect and humanity, even with those who intend to do harm, I could influence the outcome. I cannot change them, but I can help them see our shared humanity. That night, my bag was packed, and I was excited about flying away in the morning. The soldiers came for their usual raid but wanted to know who was in the house and whose packed bag it was. I explained to them that I was going away for my studies because I needed to be safe. By now, we had a routine going, and they were happy for me. They wished me well and went off to the next home.

My mom accompanied me to India, and **I was happy to leave everything behind. I had no idea which city, which school, or what life I was going to have. I was determined I was going to make it work. I had the three most valuable things in life no one can ever take away from me: my knowledge, my relationship with my God, and awareness of positively impacting the lives of others to build lasting relationships.** Along with my clothes, I carried some invisible baggage—my impenetrable walls around me, the brutal scars on my soft heart, fear, anger, and mistrust. I knew these were items I must air out and free myself of if I were to have a life of lasting peace and happiness. I was hopeful. I was Kasthuri, and I had to dig deep to find it from within me. I was going to need relationships that could help me heal.

It is true that what does not break us make us stronger. This entire journey taught me that perspective in life is key to understanding and navigating turbulent waters, no matter how deep and dark it gets. I am grateful for the opportunity to build the kind of resiliency no formal training or therapy ever could. As an adult professional, I am repeatedly asked, why don't you get upset or angry about things? How did you handle the pressures of being a young immigrant female finance executive? Didn't the stress get to you? Smiling is my instant response. I follow it up with *my life has taught me that little of how people engage with me has to do with me. When I understand that, I can stay in my Zen zone and act instead of reacting. This helps me remain relatively stress-free.* Everyone engages from their own place in life, wrapped up in their own emotions, fears, and concerns. I have learned to understand that and not react. Instead, I take the opportunity to discern where each person is coming from and what is the root cause of the issue at hand. Then, I act to address the issue. This keeps me focused on seeking to understand, effectively addressing the issue at hand, and making every engagement an inclusive process without judgment. I have found the artful balance of making sound judgments without being judgmental of the parties involved. It is like being in a meditative state in the workplace and not letting anyone take away that inner calm and balance. I use the term meditative because I am aware, I am relatable, but I am not caught up in the moment's emotions.

Another gift of this experience is the ability to understand my own emotions and the intensity of it. Then, employ the proper combination of self-management tools to address the situation at hand without getting emotional. **Adaptability to unforeseen changes, develop multiple game plans for random scenarios so as to stay ahead of circumstances, building lasting relationships I can draw from when the need arises, establishing multiple streams of income to enable economic viability in the face of fiscal challenges, continually improving my skills and capabilities to remain relevant in the employment marketplace, and artfully transforming every obstacle into a stepping stone are priceless gifts stemming from this set of experiences.** Knowing that I am in control of my life and I can figure things out with the support system open for me to lean-in is a powerful feeling. It is a contagious feeling that helps me feed off of it.

Every person I encountered in this journey has left an indelible mark on my life. It is not just success that teaches life lessons. The depth of anger, sorrow, and fear has taught me to value peace and happiness. This does not mean I have forgotten how it felt, what I lost, or how much it hurt. I have managed to learn to keep everything in perspective. These things happened. They are a part of who I am. These experiences shape me, but they no longer control me. **Nothing that happens in the US business world or society is going to shock me, given my life experience. I am continually subjected to microaggression and biases. I am told to go back to where I came from. I am dehumanized by peers and leaders because of being the other, ridiculed for my intelligence and resilience, and treated to vile comments about being married to a Caucasian man. I take it all in stride because what people think of me shows me who they are. It is not a reflection of who I am.** I have not just seen but experienced man's inhumanity to man. I have learned to expect the best from people but never failed to be prepared for the worst. By not giving power to those who harm me, I have learned to stay in control of my journey and continue to evolve into the being I was destined to become.

LESSONS LEARNED:

> ➤ **What is done to you does not define you.** *You must keep perspective to live your truth and pursue your purpose.*

> ➤ **Being aware of your environment and being in tune with the relationships is key** *to maintaining perspective for impactful solutions.*

> ➤ **You are the embodiment of your being. Do not lose yourself in pursuit of a goal.** *If you give up who you are, there is nothing left, and you have given situations control over your very essence.*

CHAPTER 6

RECAPTURING THE INNER CHILD

"There is nothing on this earth more to be prized
than true friendship."
—*Thomas Aquinas*

I chose to go to school in Bangalore, a city in the state of Karnataka, South India. It was a state where Kanada was the local language with English as the official one. I did not have to fight the stereotype of how to be a Tamil Girl, as the case would have been, had I taken my mom's advice to go to school in Tamil Nadu. **I wanted a fresh start. I wanted a clean slate. I needed time and space to examine my enormous emotional baggage to understand them and find ways to deal with them.** I wanted anonymity to regroup and rebuild from the inside-out.

Mount Carmel College was an all-girls school run by the Carmelite nuns. Most students were from the area, while others were from other cities and states. Just a hand full of us were international students. All non-local students stayed at the school campus, and our accommodation was called "hostel." High school was called PUC (pre-university class) and had two years to complete. As a first-year PUC student, I was considered a "freshee," the Bangalore vernacular for a freshman student. All *freshees* in the *hostel* were terrified of the seniors. The seniors took great pleasure in capitalizing on that fear during the initial month, making the *freshees* be their errand girls. Their antics included making the *freshees* be their alarm clock by showing up outside their room and performing a rendition of cock-a-doodle-doo, fetching them bed coffee (serving early morning coffee in bed), entertaining them after school, and other silly things.

Having just escaped a civil war, this was utterly hilarious to me. Every time they summoned me, I would show up giggling. They were surprised I was not afraid. They had also never met a Sri Lankan girl. I was an enigma. A foreign girl who always smiled, was never afraid, friendly, but never lost her cool, no matter what was said. I was summoned to one of the rooms of the seniors where about a dozen of them were gathered. They decided to teach me a lesson. I was told, "Hey *freshee*, cut your smile, kneel down, bury it, and pray for its soul." I found this to be utterly ridiculous, but I did it. As I wiped my smile, I kept a serious face and completed the instructions. Then, I promptly stood up and started talking with them. That was the start of a pleasant friendship rooted in respect to girls my age. I had earned their trust and respect by following the "coming of age process" without being combative but keeping my dignity. I was already putting my vast experience of a short childhood into good use. I decided anonymity was a good thing. I did not have to live up to any expectations. I set my own course.

There was another foreign student in my class who was able to successfully navigate this initiation with a good sense of humor. I was intrigued by this girl's personality and presence. She looked like me, her dad's name was the same as mine, and she saw the humor in situations that made situations light-hearted. I had to get to know this girl. Susila Kulasingam was from Malaysia, but her grandparents had immigrated from Sri Lanka to Malaysia. We were both Tamil girls, but the difference was she was educated in English and I was educated in Tamil. We both came from the British system of education and had just completed our GCE O/Ls. We both came from Tamil culture, raised in a society where there is no family last names. Everyone had their own name. So, we both had taken our father's names as our last names. When translated in English, she spelled it with a "K" while I did with a "G." We were both introduced to music, culture, and practices that were similar but nuanced by the home country flavor. Our similarities helped us align and understand each other better. However, we both know that there was more to us than these elements.

We both had a deep-seated sadness. Our humor was our mask for covering up that sadness. I knew it right away because I recognized what I carried within me. We also respected each other enough not to probe. Susi and I would take long walks to Brigade Road and Commercial Street on Saturdays, spend the whole day there, eat out, watch a movie, and walk back to the hostel. Saturday was our only full day out with a requirement to be on campus at dusk. We respected the rules. Growing up in a country engulfed in racial tension and war, going to a Tamil movie theatre was a suicide mission because any place the minority congregated was a bombing target. I had not been to the movies in ages. **With Susi, I relearned the simple joys of life. We did not need words to be exchanged to understand or hear each other. We connected at a deeper level. We both enjoyed our philosophical conversations, our love of food and nuanced flavors, music, movies, and more. Thus started a friendship that was to last a lifetime, despite the geographic divide and independent lives.**

Susi and I had our first sausage and egg pizza at Max, a local western pub and fast food combination place. We would try out traditional Indian street food and venture into local restaurants to experience the local flavors. We stood out in town because of the way we looked and carried ourselves; this caused a following of young men always trying to follow us around. We laughed and giggled about it, but I personally was not interested in anything. The intensity of a boy-meets-girl relationship was way too much for me, and I was not ready for any of that while I still had my invisible baggage I was lugging around. I was self-aware enough to know what not to get involved in!

Susi was a marvelous piano player and auditioned for the high school band. I was not surprised when she got selected and became the official keyboard player for the band. Her musical endeavors were a welcomed opportunity for me to be surrounded by songs I had grown up with as my escape. We even entered the high school singing competition. Our song was "Words Don't Come Easy" by F.R. David. We practiced every day and sang our hearts out. We channeled all our emotions into it. Our classmates were surprised we got up on stage and sang with heart. Of course, we did not win. But that did not stop us from having a good time. To this day, when I hear that song, I become the HS duo singer and start singing just like Susi and I did. My husband has learned to appreciate my spur-of-the-moment singing and is often amused. I can do it without a care in the world.

I will never forget the day Susi and I watched *Falling in Love* starring Meryl Streep and Robert DeNiro. A hopeless romantic at heart, Susi practically glided all the way back to the hostel while I listened to her waxing poetry about how in love she felt by the mere experience. She was a wonderful writer and had a special way of having her voice heard. I understood this because writing was my way of sharing my feelings. Robert DeNiro is my favorite Hollywood actor, thanks to this experience.

Being Susi's friend was helping me be a teenager for the first time in my life. I was learning to let my hair down, take joy in walking, sharing, enjoying the food I had not cooked, and letting go of some of the sadness. Susi is my friend for life, and she helped me take that journey of finding my inner child. We were in class and hostel together, but we had different roommates. So, our socialization was limited to after school and weekends. Since she had an older brother nearby and her mom visited her often, I had the benefit of meeting her circle. I made an instant connection with her mom, and I called her Aunty. She was unlike the aunties from Sri Lanka I was happy to get away from. I enjoyed the process of building a relationship with her that would also grow into a bond of a lifetime. As one door closed in my life, windows were opening up, and sunlight was flooding in. I felt that I was making progress.

If life was about having good friends to great adventures with, Susi and I have never stopped. We have continued to seek adventures together and hold space for each other and what matters to us. There is such calmness that comes with such a friendship. A friendship that has no pressures. A friendship that seeks to understand without being invasive. A friendship that accepts as is without reservation. A friendship that is rooted in kindness, care, and joy. A priceless gift of life to be treasured.

Over time, I learned that she had lost her father, a man she looked up to and adored. That is a loss I could not understand. I did not have that kind of relationship with my family. I listened to her and gave her my support. There were times I felt guilty of not being able to share anything because I did not know how to talk about my life and my family with anyone. Even my three roommates cried themselves to sleep every night because they missed their families. Families they talked to every week and visited often. I could not always call home, and no one visited me because there was no one for me. My roommates thought I was strong. I just let it stand with no explanation. Can sixteen-year-old girls understand what I had lived through? Was it even fair to put that burden on them and scar them for life? I chose to remain elusive and apart while remaining kind and friendly. I decided it was not my right to burden them with my circumstances. Children needed to remain children, and I was learning to be one myself.

The nuns ran a strict hostel, and we had limited funds. So, we had to be creative in finding ways to enjoy ourselves. We soon figured out that the opulent property behind the campus was a five-star hotel. While Susi was much taller than me, we were two attractive young girls who knew how to be charming. We would dress up and go to the hotel for Sunday tea. While having tea, we'd scope out what was happening that day and become engaged in the events underway. It never occurs to people to question two charming young girls. We met people, had conversations, and enjoyed some delicious food. It was fun, unpredictable, and filled our time with the excitement of a good kind. We never failed to enjoy ourselves. We even took pictures in the hotel as if we belonged there. I had gone from always being serious and responsible to daring and carefree. At that juncture in my childhood, I needed that.

We knew our time together was limited. Susi was headed to medical school, and I was pursuing a computer science, math, and physics bachelor of science. Triple majors with two languages with literature were the norm in India, and I was not trying to prove anything. I find it amusing when folks in the US tell me that I am out to prove something when they hear I have a triple major, and I am not always successful in enlightening them that that was the norm in my part of the world. Susi and I made sure we did not waste a single moment. We also knew we were going to stay connected, and geography was just a detail.

Susi had unleashed my ability to have fun and enjoy without feeling guilty. I did not have to be anyone's mother and had no responsibilities other than being focused on my education and learning to be a child. I discovered there are three apples that changed the course of human history: the apple from the Garden of Eden, Sir Isaac Newton's apple that introduced the law of gravity, and Apple computers. I have three specific individuals who shaped the course of my life history. Sr. Julia was my first, and you have already seen her profound impact on me. Susi was the second. With Susi, I learned that it is okay to have fun, enjoy life, and be the child I was capable of being without losing my sense of identity and purpose. Learning to be happy and accepting a part of me so I can be happy was my second major transformation. The third was learning to trust in the journey of meeting and marrying my husband Mike, and letting all my demons go. We will get to that in due course.

We each pursued our chosen paths and graduated. While Susi and I have never been in the same country since then, we have made time for each other and planned vacations and adventures together. We never miss a step each time we meet up. We fit into each other's lives, accepting of each other's loved ones. Susi visited me during thanksgiving to experience her first snow. We made snow angels like children and shared unvarnished joy. My husband Mike and I took Susi to the turkey farm to get our free-range Thanksgiving turkey and had a Thanksgiving meal that couldn't be beaten. On Black Friday, while everyone was caught up in Christmas shopping, we followed our new family tradition and visited Grandpa's Christmas tree farm, took a horse carriage ride, selected our tree, cut it down ourselves, and shared a cup of hot chocolate with Santa while the tree was prepared to be taken home. Susi and I decorated the tree that night and set-up our Christmas village under the tree with the train running through town.

We did not stop there. Susi climbed on our big fireplace and announced she was our good luck leprechaun. We sang carols, decorated the fireplace, and took pictures to memorialize the moment. Susi, Mike, and I have a relationship that is bound by unconditional love. Mike and I visited Susi in Australia and made a series of new memories. Watching *Carmen* be performed on the water at the Sydney Harbor, touring the Australian wine country, spending a day at the Kiama Blow Hole, watching a soccer game on TV with snacks and drinks all the while yelling at the TV, and celebrating Sri

Lankan Tamil New Year with friends were all amazing memories of one single visit. Susi and I will never stop sharing adventures. We have been good for each other not just in our childhood, but the rock-solid friendship has been the cornerstone of my ability to build a sisterhood over the years.

Even when Mike was gravely ill, Susi made sure the distance was not going to stand in the way of being a supportive friend. Always ready with medical guidance, it was a blessing to have my own medical consultant. What was even better is that she sent surprises to Mike during his recovery, so he had games and activities to engage his mind and aid in his recovery. All this has proven to me that when two people truly care about each other and commit to a lifetime of friendship, time, space, distance, career, life, or nothing else stands in the way. **Making relationships a priority is the most valuable investment with an immeasurable return on investment.** I am available for Susi to troubleshoot and guide her on decisions that have a business focus, and she does the same for me on medical matters. Two doctors, Susi being the medical doctor, and I being the finance doctor, are each other's advisors. We hold space for one another. We plan to travel, have adventures, and live with joy for as long as we can breathe. That kind of friendship is not something most people have. I, for one, am grateful for the twist of fate and divine power that brought us girls together, by chance, in a high school in Bangalore, India.

The more I embrace happiness, the sadness and pain found their place. I have never forgotten all that caused me pain. The joy of simple friendship with another teenage child healed my wounds like no other could have. It did not come from a world of psychologists and therapists. **Healing was an individual pursuit, and those who were blessed found the relationships that helped us through that healing journey.** Susi and I met each other when we were dealing with our own loss and sadness. When we bonded in that stage of our lives, we were not only able to help each other in our healing journey, and we forged a friendship that was going to sustain us for the long haul.

LESSONS LEARNED:

> ➢ *One smile, one person, one friendship can change a life and heal the wounds.* Live life in a way to notice that opportunity and lean in to be the catalyst for healing.

> ➢ *Happiness is a journey. It must be tirelessly embarked on and embraced to find lasting joy.* It is possible to find happiness, even in the darkest times, if you allow it to be sought with mindfulness.

> ➢ *Genuine friendship soothes the most broken soul, and from that healing could emerge a lasting relationship.* When such a relationship is mastered, it gives you the capability to be the constant gardener to nurture various meaningful relationships in life.

CHAPTER 7

HEALING WITH ACCEPTANCE

"Trauma creates change you don't choose. Healing is about creating change you do choose."
—Michelle Rosenthal

Living in Bangalore, India, and attending high school was a refreshing new beginning. I reveled in the anonymity and the utter freedom that accompanied it. I was able to make all my decisions starting with what I wore, what I ate, where I went, how long I walked, and how much I laughed. I attended classes Monday through Friday, eight to five, with an hour for lunch at noon. When I had arrived to arrange for admission at Mount Carmel College, I was asked to sit for an entrance exam, and the chair of the mathematics department, Ms. Shanta, grilled me with a series of questions in English. While I spoke English as if it were my native tongue, I had no clue about any technical terminologies in English for any subject matter. Ms. Shanta was concerned that I might not be a fit for the math and science curriculum I had applied for, but I reassured her to let me please take the test. A kind soul she was, took me at my word, giving me the opportunity to take the test. She graded my work right away and called me in for an interview, a rather unusual step, per the admission process. I figured I had nothing to lose and began with all the gusto I could muster.

"You have done very well on the test, but I do not understand why you did not articulate your command of the subjects when we talked earlier?" was Ms. Shanta's opening remark to me. I knew that she and I would get along wonderfully well, given our shared penchant for the direct approach. I took my time to explain that my education thus far had been in Tamil, and I do all my schoolwork in my own language. I also sought her guidance on how to transition from a Tamil language classroom to English. This was the start of a mentor-mentee relationship Ms. Shanta and I embarked on. She never failed to keep an eye on me and make space for me in her professional life, so I had a safe place to discuss academic concerns. Ms. Shanta took up where Sr. Julia had left off. The universe was unfolding as it should, and I felt my academic life was off to a reasonable start.

The first day of class was a whole new experience. I had never had to take notes in English and did not understand the technical terms for any of the subject matters. Algebra, geometry, trigonometry, calculus, physics, chemistry, botany, and zoology all sounded Greek. **Frustrated, I started taking notes in Tamil, making sure when I read my Tamil notes, it sounded like the English words used in class. That evening, I sat in my hostel room with an English-Tamil dictionary and glossary of terms for each subject to translate my phonetically written notes into proper English notes. Painful as it was, this cumbersome process over the course of the first few months helped me transition effectively to be proficient in class.** The focus and single-mindedness required to master this challenging transition gave me little time to be carefree, except with my friend Susi on weekends. This experience taught me the full suite of self-management skills and how to best employ them purposefully. Today, when folks ask me how I do all the things I do and still succeed, I can smile and silently thank my transformational journey in India with the guidance of Ms. Shantha!

My two pre-university years flew by with my adjustment to living in a new country, adapting to the local culture, learning the local state language, "Kannada," and building new relationships and having Susi as my friend made things joyful. I shared my hostel room with three other girls. One of the girls was Anglo-Indian with Portuguese ancestry. The other two girls were from Mizoram, a northeastern state in India with larger Chinese influence in food and social perspectives. I got a rich and expansive exposure to my new temporary home. I began to understand how diverse and vibrant India is. I was also observing how such a large democracy, with its massive humanity, held a nation together, celebrating its inherent diversity. The common official language of English helped accomplish that.

The food served at the hostel was not at all flavorful. I had been cooking meals for my family for a few years, and I missed the aromas. My roommates and I soon realized that if we did not eat the food, the uneaten portions got recycled into the next meal in a different form. As wasteful as our solution was, we served as much as we could fill in each of our plates and mixed eggshells and uneaten food together to ensure they never saw a cooking utensil again. This meant we were hungry by 7:00 p.m. Our warden, Sr. Juaneta, had her room just two doors down from my room. She ran a small snack store so we could buy cookies and snacks to hold us over.

Sr. Juaneta was a remarkably interesting nun. She was young and curious but also stern and serious. On her room door, she had a sign posted for all of us to see, which read, "All my visitors bring me happiness. Some by coming and *others by going."* This message always gave me pause. I certainly did not want to make her happy by leaving because it meant my presence was unbearable. This also taught me a nuanced perspective. **All people who enter and exit my life can make me happy—some by coming into it, and others by exiting it. This has been a pragmatic reminder when I have to deal with rude, crude, and overtly prejudiced individuals because I know I was going to be happy when I figured out how to exit them from my sphere of life.**

Not one for processed food and having limited spending money due to my lack of access to funds, I refrained from purchasing items from Sr. Juanita's hostel store. Susi and I figured out that we could sweet-talk the canteen ladies into making us egg sandwiches for a few rupees. Since I taught the nuns computer programming, they gave me fish every Friday. The students got the head and tail of the fish, and we had always wondered what happened to the whole body of the fish. Once I started getting Friday fish pieces, the light bulb went on. We also made friends with the woman who was raising her two children in the ditch across the street from our campus entrance. For a rupee each, she would roast fresh corn, locally referred to as "butta," with ground green chilies and lime. This quenched my yearning for flavor and gave me the opportunity to get to know the family. Our campus was across the street from the Bangalore Palace. Behind us was a five-star hotel. Down the street was the slum. Across the street was the butta lady. This was a direct reflection of Indian society at large, a stark disparity between the haves and have-nots.

Every one of these relationships touched me in some way, teaching me life lessons and helping me become socially aware. I always remembered how blessed I was, in spite of all that life had put in my path thus far. **Here were women of different worlds, teaching me things that would come to shape my adult journey with an acute awareness of the need for social justice and equity.** All women, doing the best they can, making sacrifices in their own way to take care of her children and children of others. **It was a humbling experience**

to realize one did not have to be rich or well-healed to touch the lives of young people. It was a reality check to comprehend that if I did not choose to continually be in the moment and see with my heart, I would miss all that the world around me had to offer.

Doing research in multiple languages was a plus in university, and we were required to have two language selected as part of our higher education. I chose English and Tamil so I could continue to remain steeped in my own heritage and benefit from the rich traditions and knowledge dating back to 5th century BC. During my first class for the Tamil language, my professor and classmates assumed that I would struggle with the material as a foreign student. **By the time I was a teenager, I had learned to let others underestimate me because, by doing so, they are giving me the ultimate power when I decide to demonstrate my competencies and abilities. I had nothing to lose and everything to gain by letting matters take their natural course. I had learned not to get mad but get even.** The first class assignment at the end of the week was an essay on what I imagine God to be. Having had a foundational education in Sri Lanka steeped in religious philosophies and understanding the interconnectedness of Hinduism with science, I loved the challenge this essay offered me. I started writing.

I addressed the intersection of Hinduism and science. In Hinduism, Shiva, the dancing male God, symbolizes the movement of an atom, and his female counterpart, Shakthi, literally means energy. The union of atom and energy, Shiva and Shakthi, created this universe. Everything around us, including ourselves, is an embodiment of that union. While the bodies go through the process of birth, growth, and death, the soul comes from the energy source that is omnipotent and ever-present. That is why Hindus put their palms together and greet each other saying, "Vanakkam," or, "Namaste." It means, **"I see the light in you that is of truth, love, and peace. When I see you in that place of light, we are one."** I also understood that in that place, science and

Hinduism unite, as an energy that can neither be created nor destroyed. It unites us all, regardless of where we come from and what our faith is. I went on to explain how the process of death is when the energy embodied by the soul leaves the body and enters the new cycle through re-birth. I talked about how we are all a part of the all-powerful energy source I call God, a God that is neither male nor female but embodies all genders. A God that is not defined by any specific religion but embodied all of spirituality, holding space for the various religions and religious interpretations. A God that is the source of energy of the universe that sustains life. Just like all rivers flow toward the ocean, all religions speak of the same God. A God who is everywhere and in all things. I see God's presence in all things and beings. **We are all a part of our creator and of our creator. In that place of recognition, I see science and spirituality come together and coexist in harmony, giving my life meaning and purpose to honor all that is around me and of me.**

That was the last day I ever had to sit through a Tamil class. My professor read my Tamil essay out loud to the class. There was pin-drop silence. The professor advised me that there was nothing he was going to teach in the class that would be new to me, and I should use that time to focus on some other subject I needed to learn. All I had to do is take the exams as they came due. I did not know what to say or do. It was never my intent to show off or make anyone feel less than. I was merely demonstrating my mastery of the language and the subject matter. I was well-read and steeped in literature to a point where I could quote my sources from memory. I was afraid I had upset my professor. So, I approached him after class and shared my concern. He gently told me that my Tamil language skills were exceptional, and the fact that I had done all my education in Tamil showed. There were no more grammar, literature, writing, or comprehension skills I needed to master, and he respected me to let me focus on areas I needed to invest time in.

That day, I moved from being my Tamil professor's student to his friend and colleague at the age of seventeen. He came to me for advice on Tamil, and my classmates came to me for help with the language. **It is okay for the teacher to become the student and the student to become the teacher because learning is never unidirectional. We all have something to learn from everybody. What a valuable lesson learned from the humility of my professor.** I knew that was the kind of person I wanted to be when I grow up: humble enough to recognize talent and honor that talent by willing to be transformed by it.

For my bachelor's degree, the computer science project was a team deliverable and a requirement for graduation. A four-member team had to pick a topic and develop the necessary automation to meet the requirement of the client. The test for final grade included the examiners testing the client's ability to use the solution developed and the usefulness of the solution in running of their business. My team chose to automate the university library using C+ programming. We were going to modernize our library and rollout the automation solution to improve the lives of all future students. We were going to leave a legacy in the place that was building us to embrace the future that awaited us. Rupa and Asha were two of the local students who came to class from home. They were also my teammates. We decided to work on the project from their homes and spent time away from the hostel researching, brainstorming, coding, and testing. Both Rupa's and Asha's families were so very welcoming of me.

Asha's mom always had a warm meal for me and taught me all the Hindi I continue to muddle my way through to this day. Between our made-up sign language and me learning Hindi, Aunty and I communicated. My introduction to North Indian food was thanks to Asha and her mom. I was even included in her brother's wedding, where I got to stay over and enjoy the multi-day celebrations while being introduced to their traditions. I looked forward to getting on the bike with Asha and heading to her home for her mom to treat me to a feast.

Rupa's parents were scientists, and they spoke Tamil. They, too, opened up their home to me and welcomed me with no questions asked. I remember quietly sitting on the swing on their front porch and enjoying the meditative peacefulness. I can honestly say that when I think back to my childhood, Uncle and Aunty Krishna's front porch swing chair is my place of peace. Never once did they grill me with any questions. They just embraced me and held space for me. We talked in Tamil to my heart's content, and Rupa giggled at my use of pure Tamil with no English substitutions.

Asha and Rupa were integral in my continued healing process because through them, I had two families that accepted me just as I was. I was good enough as I was. They did not have to grill me with questions in an interrogation style, and they did not have to change me to fit their definition of who I ought to be. This was not the case with any other young woman who befriended me and invited me home. India, unfortunately, is a country that is not safe for women, regardless of age. Men looked for opportunities to take advantage of a woman, regardless of age. Brothers and fathers of classmates and friends could be dangerous. I had to tread carefully. Especially since as I entered university, I had brought my younger sister to Bangalore with me to help her pursue her high school education. I was responsible for my sixteen-year-old sister while I was just eighteen.

Always serious about my duty and responsibility, I took my sister's protection seriously. I always carried a bag of hot chili peppers and an open safety pin to protect myself and my sister from unwanted attention. I did not hesitate to use them when the situation called for it. I had learned to jump into running busses and trains to secure seats so I could let my sister sit by the window while I took the aisle and stay guard. The super vigilance growing up in the war zone and protecting my younger sister as far back as I can remember just took on its natural evolution. Now, I was her mother, father, and protector. **Looking back, I wonder if I took my other roles so seriously that I failed in being her sister. She had grown**

to depend on me, and I focused on protecting her. Today, I have made peace with the fact that I was a child raising a child. I did the best I could.

My friend's father threw me out of the home on a weekend night because his son called in sick to work and stayed back to help me upholster their family sofa as a gift to the family. I was accused of enticing the son and trying to trap him into matrimony as well as turning the docile daughter into an independent young woman. I had apparently caused shame to my friend's family. My sister and I were thrown out with no place to go, late at night. At that time, I was hurt and devastated. I checked into a hotel for the weekend. With all my money gone to pay for the hotel room, I had no money for food. I had to improvise. Milk and eggs were cheap in India. So, I bought plenty of both. We both had out-baths until we emptied the hot water heater in the bathroom. Then, we carefully placed all the eggs in the heater tank and refilled it with water for heating. Every time we were hungry, we had a bath to empty the hot water and ate our new hardboiled eggs, and followed up with milk. I was proud of the creative solution I had devised!

That weekend, I made arrangements to rent a room with a kitchen for my sister and me. We walked to school, taught the children from the slums after class, bought groceries on our walk home, and cooked dinner. The extra dinner became lunch for the next day in school. The main house was occupied by an empty-nester British couple who had a carriage house with a young family to attend the needs of the main house. Priscilla and Jayanath were a wonderful couple with a young boy with polio and a daughter full of life. After observing my schedule for a week, Priscilla made arrangements with the owner to serve my sister and me breakfast on the house. She could not allow a child to get up at 4:00 a.m. to cook and clean before going to school, then work, grocery shop, come home to cook dinner, clean up, then study late into the night. Here was a woman who cared about me, a stranger, and took it upon herself to make my life a bit better. The rich owner who rented me the room did not even notice. **Priscilla was a**

maid by profession. Jayanath was the caretaker of the property. Together, they became my lifeline. In their eyes, I was not an outsider. I was not the other. I was a child who needed support. While they had nothing, they found a way to nurture me and be my rock. They were instrumental in teaching me *how we treat others is the true reflection of who we are*.

My father had tried to send money whenever he could, and due to the war, there was no direct way to send money. He had to give money to businessmen coming to India, and I had to pick it up from them. The first time such an arrangement was made, I was asked to come to a hotel room to collect money. I was already gun shy. The situation did not sit well with me. I left my sister behind and took two friends. I made arrangements with an auto-rickshaw driver from the slums, someone I trusted. He was going to drive all three of us to the hotel. One of the girls would stay in the auto-rickshaw while the other friend went with me to the hotel. She was to stand by the hotel room doorway, keeping the door open. I was going to go in, get the money, and leave. As I entered the hotel room, I saw an empty red label Johnny Walker bottle on the table and a drunk man sitting by it, telling me what I needed to do to get the money he had for me from my father. Thank God I had a good grasp of geometry and physics. I triangulated how fast I had to move and what trajectory I had to take to snatch the money without letting him grab me and run. Fear was not an emotion I dwelled on. My childhood had taught me to channel fear into actionable solutions so as to never be paralyzed. At that moment, I was grateful for a hard lesson I learned as a child. It was also my blessing that this businessman was not steady and was drunk. I was an athlete with both endurance and strength. I could take on an older drunk man. I had seen in American movies where to kick so any man could not move for a few minutes. My quick assessment made, and execution plan formulated, I sprang into action. The element of surprise was on my side, and I ran out with the money along with my friend at the doorway. That was the last day I ever agreed to go pick up any money my father sent through businessmen. I was relieved that my friends were safe, and we made a promise never to allow any of us to get in that position again. It was too risky, and we may never get lucky a second time.

My friends and classmates, Meera, Sapna, Jeeva, Priya, Sara, et al., were part of my growing up. We enjoyed our time together working, studying, and being playful. We were mischievous in class, made life challenging to our professors, caused trouble, and did all the things young adults do as part of coming of age. There was never a dull moment with these girls. I was still guarded about my life and history because I did not want to burden anyone with it. I also did not know how to talk about any of that. I had not yet sorted things out for myself. These young women embraced me, and with them, I belonged. Sure, there were challenges and roadblocks. There were heartache and undue pressure. However, my glass was half full, and I embrace that with a grateful heart.

When I look back at the Indian community that accepted me as I was, included me in their daily lives without forcing me to change, and stood up as my support system purely because that was the right thing to do, I feel nothing but respect and love. While I have never had the opportunity to return to Bangalore, I look forward to it in the near future. My friends have stayed in touch with me. Uncle and Aunty Krishnan even visited me in Chicago. Asha and I exchange messages often. Meera has become a renowned figure dedicated to Bangalore's history. Each of these young women has become mothers, professionals and remained friends. **Genuine and lasting relationships are bonds of the soul and engage the heart. There is no need for proximity or material exchange.** Bangalore was my place of peace and my circle during those years ennobled my transformation to help me become the person I am today. I got my technical education there that catapulted me to success in the field of international finance via FinTech. I found my purpose and mastered the art of building lasting relationships in that beautiful garden city. **Bangalore is the place I became a butterfly and learned**

to fly free. I still had baggage to unload, but my flight had taken off, and I was empowered to land on my destiny.

Being able to integrate technology with finance and build successful business relationships are what allowed me to become a young CFO. Today, everything I do is technology-driven. Learning to let go of fear and anger, learning to meet others where they are, and holding space for others is part of who I am today because of my days in Bangalore. Learning to live after a prolonged trauma is not an easy feat, but it is possible. Because of the support of an entire community of people who did not know me from Adam, I had the power to decide how my healing would take shape. Today, I pay it forward by holding space for others. It is amazing how the universe connects the right people. Not a week goes by where random strangers don't reach out to me to talk or get guidance. I am told that I am easy to talk to and am uniquely kind.

We live in a world where men, more so than women, have fewer options to have a safe conversation. My ability to be there for men and women alike, in a nurturing way, is a gift I am paying forward with gratitude. I get told that I should charge people for help and should stop talking to strangers. I understand that it is a normal fear for folks in the US. I am from another world. I am living proof that strangers can walk into a life and heal the wounds if allowed. I cannot monetize that human connection. My time with unconditional nurturing is a priceless gift I can give in honor of all that was given to me, by so many, over the course of five years. Love and kindness only have value when they are given away unconditionally. That is the kind of value the soul could grasp, but the wallet would never fathom.

Lessons Learned:

➢ *Every human interaction is an opportunity for transformation.* How we make it possible is predicated on being open with the ability to meet others where they are and keeping an open mind.

➢ *Humility is a superpower that offers the opportunity to lean in and seek help from others.* None of us are going to make through this life alone, and we need our fellow travelers in each of our healing journeys.

➢ *Most valuable things in life cannot be bought, and helping others when you have nothing is the ultimate definition of love.* Putting a price on kindness and humanity is unbecoming. Selfless love can never be repaid; it can only be paid forward to pass on the legacy of those who made our lives possible.

CHAPTER 8

FINDING PEACE THROUGH SERVICE

"Service to man is service to God."
—*Hindu Proverb*

In the early days in Bangalore, I would walk down the streets around the school, after classes, to clear my mind and get to know the community. I was naturally a friendly young person, and strangers readily engaged with me. I started observing the children and families living in a slum not too far from my school. For some reason, I identified with them and established a relationship with them. In a way, I felt just as disenfranchised and alone as they were. I learned that they needed help with school and were bright young people who could thrive academically. I had a plan to build something good for them and me. I had to get the permission of the nuns to put my idea into practice.

I proposed to the nuns that I tutor some of the kids from the slum on school property after my classes end. I told them that it would help me practice my English, and since most of those children spoke Tamil, it would be a good bonding experience for all of us. The nuns thought that was a good way to serve the community and gave me permission to tutor the kids five days a week. The parents of the kids were incredibly happy, and I became the big sister, "Akka," to these children. I learned to integrate culturally through these interactions and found the whole experience very fulfilling. The school system in India encouraged volunteer work by students who benefitted from taxpayer funding. Social work or volunteer military training were the two areas that were encouraged. Foreign students have not traditionally pursued either of these, but I was the exception. In all honesty, I was not doing it to get any credit; I was doing it to have a sense of belonging.

Very soon, my afterschool tutoring program became popular, and more and more kids from the slum started coming. We would stay and then play. The nuns valued my contribution and allowed me to start teaching in the computer lab as well. I learned to use the computer and then ran classes for other students. The nuns got fee training from me as well. The nuns paid me, so I had money to pay for school. **It was my first win-win-win deal negotiated and brought to life. The school won because it was a community-building endeavor; the children won because they were thriving in school; I won because I was finding my purpose and earning money.** I have carried this win-win strategy into adulthood to make sustainable decisions as a business leader.

One of my students topped the class, and her school wanted to honor me at their school assembly for being the tutor. In appreciation for my tireless work, the adults in the slum pooled their resources and bought me my first pair of jeans and a t-shirt. It was the first pair of jeans I ever owned.

I proudly wore that gift from their heart and attended the school assembly. I felt like I had won the lottery that day. I knew I will always be involved in teaching and serving because that was my purpose. These children and their families did not have much, but they embraced me into their families. They sent me homemade treats and made me feel at home. I belonged with them. No judgment. Just acceptance.

There were school holidays and vacations, but due to the war back home, I had no place to go. I would volunteer to build roads and schools in rural India as part of the National Social Service Program. I met Indian students from all over the country and learned their music, dancing, and food preparation. Everyone was accepting of me and appreciated the fact that I was a foreign student engaged in giving back to the country that had given me a home. I was not a refugee. I was a contributing young person with purpose and relationships. I continued my engagement with the National Social Service (NSS) into my bachelor's degree, always looking forward to learning something new and building meaningful relationships.

Dodderi was our chosen village to build a school one year, a small community in the state of Karnataka. Rural India was highly steeped in tradition, and as a foreigner, I needed to respect their tradition and accept it. Part of that acceptance meant that I had to honor their caste system. While I was a Hindu amongst other Hindus, I did not come from a society that had a caste system. In India, the caste system was strictly adhered to. That meant I could not be housed with any villagers because I had no caste to fit into. The village had a solution. They set up my space with the cows in their barn. I understood that this is a community that worshipped the cow, and, therefore, I was being allowed into a sacred space to cohabit with the cows. I did not find this demeaning because I understood their culture and had a respectful perspective of why this was a good option. Morning ablutions were playfully referred to as fieldwork by me, and I was given the space and time to attend to myself. I continued to visit Dodderi throughout my stay in India and built a wonderful relationship with the local community. The children came running, lined up, and saluted to me each morning. My *Kannada*, the local language, was not very fluent, and I taught them English. That meant they greeted me like they see Westerners greet with a salute. The kids loved doing it, and I played along to salute back.

These simple villages and the families in the slum taught me the meaning of unconditional acceptance. Today, I can walk into any boardroom, business meeting, or social setting and be myself without reserve because these communities taught me how to walk with purpose and own the space I occupy without the need to explain or apologize. Learning, caring, sharing, and ennobling does not have to come from money, power, and position. It can only come from a place of love, acceptance, care, and kindness. They showed me how to remain centered in that kindness even when we did not share a common language. I learned how to be different and still belong. Thirty years later, I carry a part of these communities in my soul, for they were an integral part of my healing and ennobling.

I got to work with Indian students from other universities as we traveled across the country and worked on NSS projects. During one such NSS camp, I contracted jaundice. The intersection of the rural community, infectious disease, and superstition made for a remarkable experience. I was first isolated and given specific herbal concoctions to consume. They also burned leaves and performed rituals around me to ward away evil spirits while the nuns sat around me, saying the rosary. As a young person, I enjoyed the entertainment and had a good laugh. While I was sick, the zeal with which everyone focused on me and did everything they believed in with such earnestness only made me appreciate them. There was no doctor in sight, but I did recover, giving more power to the rituals and natural healing.

Working with students from different states and communities exposed me to their food, music, and dancing. These were beautiful bonding experiences. I naturally gravitated to the Punjabi folk music and dancing. The Bhangra music and dancing could get me on my feet and dance any day, any time. I had grown up learning traditional Bharatanatyam dancing and Karnaatic music. I used to sign at the Hindu temple for the holidays and played the violin. All of that was more choreographed and highly technical. Bhangra dancing, on the other hand, reminded me of pure expression of joy. It helped me forget the trauma; it helped me enjoy the moment, and it helped me grow comfortable in mixed company. There was friendship, respect, and unbridled joy. My fellow Sikh male students grabbed tree branches so I could hold one end while they held the other whenever we had to walk on uneven terrain or cross rivers. These handsome young men were raised to treat the opposite gender with respect and protect them. It was a welcome change for my tired heart. It gave me hope for the goodness out there.

Locally, in Bangalore, we volunteered at a senior living home where older Europeans with no immediate families in the country resided. Our volunteer work included doing crafts with them, reading for them, helping them with their self-care, and, at times, helping them get dressed for a date or play games. These weekend outings gave me the opportunity to have surrogate grandparents. I loved the bonding opportunity and hearing their stories. It was the ladies in the senior living home who started calling me "Kas" because, for their British and Portuguese native tongues, "Kasthuri" was too complicated. I did not mind that they shortened my name. I looked at it as their name of endearment for me.

Through these various social and community interactions, I was gaining a deeper understanding of how a compassionate society could craft a sustainable program where students benefitted from taxpayer-funded education could give back to society in impactful ways. We were all responsible for one another. We did not need money to solve all our problems. All we needed was compassion, willingness, and follow-through. Both Sri Lanka and India, as developing countries, had this figured out. I never realized the power of such social exchange programs until I came to the US and started seeing how every problem has a solution that required funding. There is never enough money, and money cannot solve all social problems.

I keep going back to the poem about how the kingdom was lost for want of a nail. I knew that understanding the root cause was the first step to solve any problem, including social problems. When I ask why the kingdom was lost, the answer is because the message was not delivered on time. The message was not delivered on time because the knight died. The knight died because the horse got hurt. The horse was hurt because the horseshoe failed for want of a nail. What was wrong with the nail? If the nail was forgotten, it was a process and quality assurance problem. If there was a shortage of nails, it is a raw material or supply chain problem. In order to prevent other kingdoms from getting lost, one needs to ensure process, quality, resource availability, and supply chain viability. Applying this logic, one could understand that not all social problems can be solved by throwing money at it.

Money does not solve all our problems is a fact of life that is often lost in the US way of life. As a corporate financial strategist consulting in the space of mergers, acquisitions, and organizational restructuring, I get to apply root-cause analysis for problem-solving and simplification for process waste reduction. I find myself drawing from my social service experience to ask why, why, and more why, until the true root of the problem is identified. Being the eternal three-year-old asking parents, "Why?" and "Are we there yet?" are two important questions in the world of waste reduction, quality assurance, simplification, and problem-solving.

That same approach can be used in public sector problem-solving. When I teach my US military and public safety professionals, I am always showing them how to use data to identify the root of problems and then formulate solutions that are sustainable with the exploration of how to accomplish the follow-through, keeping money as a constrain. Is food insecurity a problem that requires money when one part of the population throws food away while another is starving? An ideal example is that farmers and businesses were throwing away produce and meat amidst the pandemic, while over 15 million people became newly unemployed and struggled to feed their families. Why couldn't the richest country in the world find an effective way to establish a supply chain that would have created jobs and feed the starving? Is it a smart move for one group to throw food while the policymakers argue over how much money should be given to the unemployed and for how long? I wish to see a day in the US where the blueprint from India and Sri Lanka are implemented, where what is in our own ecosystem can help our communities.

Serving the community that gave me a home for the most critical five years of my young life was not something I had to do. I did it because it gave me joy and helped me find my peace. It also gave me perspective. As a finance leader and finance professor, I take my life lessons into the classroom. **We have two United States of America. One that is at the top of the global economic pyramid, while the other at the bottom of the pyramid. This means the solution that works for the top 1 percent is never going to work for those at the bottom. Why not bring strategies for the bottom of the pyramid from the developing world as solutions for the US?** I am encouraged that the younger generation will be more open to exploring such viable win-win solutions, even as the older generation resists the change. Conscious capitalism had the inherent ability to integrate this thinking, making equity front and center.

Equity is different from equality. Equality expects everyone to be treated the same. Let us take, for example, a mom who takes her three-year-old and one-year-old to the community swimming pool. Can she assume that since all three of them were at the pool, she can go about her enjoyment without caring or supporting her children? Equality requires just that. Give the same opportunity, and then let things take their own course. Equity, on the other hand, requires the mother to make sure the three-year-old is helped to get into the shallow end and play safely before carrying the one-year-old into the pool with her and introducing the baby to the water while holding it. Each person should be supported and facilitated to take part in the experience. **Social work and community engagement helped me understand, through exposure and experiential learning, the namesake approach equality was, and the lasting impact equity brought about.**

Along with a bachelor's in computer science, math, and physics, I was awarded a diploma in social service by Bangalore University. It was not a qualification I actively pursued. I got involved in the experience to have a place to be, something meaningful to contribute toward and build meaningful relationships. I am often told by business leaders that my qualifications and awards are intimidating, and I should keep them hidden. Most folks do not take a moment to inquire or understand where all those came from or why. They have made up their mind that I am a qualification collector. If they care enough to ask or engage in a genuine conversation, they could learn a few things. But that is not the point at hand here. The point is that my university valued my contribution and recognized my work.

When I graduated in 1991, I earned two awards. One was the Most Outstanding Student of the Year, a traditional award given away. The other was Most Socially Aware Student of the Year, a special award custom-created to recognize all my contributions to Indian society through my social work. I was humbled by this experience and twice blessed when the younger sister I had raised in India by myself was awarded it two years later with the explicit citation that she was taking home an award established from the recognition of her older sister's legacy.

Lessons Learned:

➤ **The ability to accept without judgment and include everyone establishes the foundation for success.** Success is accomplished only through supportive collaboration because life is not a solo sport, but a team endeavor.

➤ **Different cultures communicate differently, and recognizing it allows for a fruitful experience.** Growing beyond the pre-judging and not giving into bias-based stereotyping leads to extraordinary results.

➤ **Ennobling others is the gift from the heart given freely by anyone who has the capacity to care.** It is not the prerogative of the elite or those in power.

CHAPTER 9

BUILDING BONDS FROM THE ASHES

"Fear is the path to the dark side. Fear leads to anger, anger leads to hate, and hate leads to suffering."
—Yoda

Once I completed my education in India, I had to return home to Sri Lanka. It was not a matter of choice. It was immigration and visa control requirements. During the five years in Bangalore, I had the opportunity to evolve into the young adult I wanted to be, but my transformation had not yet concluded. I had miles to go but now had more tools at my disposal to courageously embrace the journey ahead. I knew once I entered Sri Lanka, I would lose touch with all my Indian friends who had become family. We said our goodbyes and promised to find each other, someday, somehow. My sister had two more years of her degree to be completed, and my support system was going to protect her and guide her through her life. The most heart-breaking moment was when my sister hid behind the vehicle that brought me to the airport, sobbing her heart out. It was then that I realized how attached she had become to having me around and taking care of her. Now, she had to take care of things on her own. I was hopeful that she had the start and connections needed to take flight and soar.

Getting a job and establishing a career while exploring options for a permanent transition out of Sri Lanka was my plan. A plan I shared with no one. By now, I was used to keeping my own council and strategically developing my plans to protect myself. I knew I was headed somewhere; I knew the journey continues. I just did not know when, where, or how. I knew that as long as I remained open to the opportunities the universe presented, my path will get shaped. I just had to embrace each day to its fullest and put my best self out there without fear or reservation. **When I landed at the Katunayaka International Airport, Sri Lanka, I was ready to take the leap of faith and continue down my road least traveled. I reasoned, what is the worst thing that could happen to me? Death. In such a case, my soul would be reborn to fulfill its destiny, and I had nothing to worry about, as I will cease to dwell in this body. If not, I will still be alive, and I will find a way.** This logical reasoning became my go-to self-talk to sustain me through all of life's challenges. Even today, I am told that I have an interesting perspective and relationship with my own death. While it surprises others, especially because I verbalize it with sincerity and humor, it never fails to put things in perspective for me.

Looking for a job as a foreign graduate and Tamil was an interesting experience. I looked through the employment section of the newspaper and applied for open positions. One day, I saw the opening for management trainees for a British bank on the island—a bank my father had worked for and retired from nearly ten years prior before moving to the Middle East to work. They were looking for individuals with university degrees and a willingness to learn. I decided to apply and presented my best case in writing, outlining the value I could bring to the international bank to transform its operation and help their journey into the FinTech era as one of the first batches of technology graduates from Bangalore University.

I was called in for a face-to-face interview. I knew I had made the first cut. Now, I had to be persuasive in my interview. I knew there would be the British Country Leadership Team, a team that rotated in and out every two to four years with no history of anything or anyone who was there prior to their arrival. I also knew there would be some of the Sri Lankan management team members who knew my father, some who liked him, and some who did not. I was also conscious that I was Tamil, and that could be negative, depending on how these individuals viewed the civil war. I needed to discern their biases and show up as a being, transcending my ethnicity without selling out.

I always took pride in dressing in my traditional saree, the Tamil Hindu attire. I looked good in it, and it allowed me to feel feminine while I hold my ground and speak my truth boldly. I wore a hunter green saree with a bright pink contrasting border and headpiece with a matching blouse. My black wavy hair, loose with earrings, and "pottu" as my adornment, along with makeup completed the look. "Pottu" was a dot that Hindu women wear on our foreheads to remind us and others that no matter who is present or absent, there is always the third eye, the all-seeing eye of God, watching us. And to remind us of the karmic impact of our words and action. Married women wore red, and others wore black. **I knew I looked good, and I felt fabulous, ready to take on my interview. I had nothing to lose and everything to gain.**

As I was waiting to be called into the interview, the young lady interviewing just ahead of me came running out of the conference room with her saree falling apart. I did not stop to think but jumped onto my feet and guided her into the adjoining room. While we introduced ourselves to each other, I helped her get the saree back on in her beautiful Kandyan style. There is a unique way Sinhala women drape their saree, which was rather different from how I, as a Tamil woman, did. For that moment, I forgot I was in the next interview. I let my instincts of helping a young woman in distress take precedence. Once she was comfortable and could step out, we both walked out together and continued with the interview process without missing a beat. The hiring manager and the management team observed all this, making their own mental notes on things an interview would never reveal. This young woman and I have remained friends all these years later. We have grown professionally and personally, but the bond that was formed in that instant proved that when the chips are down, our humanity can triumph.

During my interview, I was asked why I thought I should have the position of management trainee. I was the youngest applicant at twenty-two years of age. A natural storyteller, I told them a story about the young Kasthuri. *When I was a child of a banker who worked for this office, I had the good fortune of attending your bank's annual Christmas party for the children. I watched Santa arrive with such awe and delighted in the celebrations. As a ten-year-old, I gave the thank you speech on behalf of the children to the management team for including all of us and making our evening special. The country manager at that time pulled me aside after my speech and told me that if I ever want to come and work for the bank, the job was mine, but I had to first go and get myself a good education.* They were all intently listening to my story, and I told them that I have now returned with a degree that can help the bank enter the technology era by taking up the offer made to me twelve years ago! At first, there was stunned silence because no one saw that coming. It was not something I had pre-planned because I had no idea what they would ask me. As I sat there, holding their gaze without looking away, with a sweet smile, they started laughing and told me what a novel answer that was.

They also had to admit that it took guts to walk in here and claim the offer, twelve years later.

When the interview concluded, I knew I had the job. I was not surprised when I got the official offer. The bank recruited five management trainees. We were all women. One Tamil, one Muslim, and three Sinhala Buddhists. Diversity was not a conscious movement on the island because employers focused on talent and business continuity. I was the only technology graduate. We went through all six functional areas of the bank: IT, ForEx, remittance, clearing, retail, and corporate banking, over the course of six months to learn the banking operations in a holistic manner. Having been out of the country, I had to adjust and adapt to the working world of Colombo, Sri Lanka. I decided, in order to be successful as a banker, I needed to sit for the banking exams and earn the credentials. True to form, I sat for the full exam at one time and passed. The bank recognized my efforts and awarded me a Rs10,000 cash bonus. This was novel to me. I made a good salary compared to most working adults, and I was only twenty-two years of age. On top of that, I earned a bonus, which was exciting. I started saving.

When it came time to start a new branch in a Tamil community in Colombo, I was tapped to be a part of the startup team. The team was mainly comprised of young professionals, and most of us were single. This experience of starting up a new branch operation, running it as a team, working with individuals around my age, and building something that would help the community, was highly rewarding. By then, I was twenty-three. The bank had clerical ranks that were union employees and the management rank, which was not. All managers came up from the unionized clerical ranks. I was the exception, having joined directly into management. Culturally, there was no animosity or divide between union and management. Everyone had the opportunity to grow into management roles. It took me coming to the US to realize union-management harmony was not a given.

I was learning to build community relationships, serving clients of all ethnicities, and conversing with clients in all three languages: Tamil, Sinhala, and English. It was a rich experience, and I lived in that community. The same fishermen at the top of my street who protected our lives in 1983 were still selling fish in that street corner. They called me "Baby" because I will always be a child in their eyes, and I appreciated it, knowing they cared about me and loved me to protect me. They would stand up and greet me every morning as I walked a few blocks to work. If I was running late, I would take the bus, but a brisk walk was good to clear my mind and prepare for work. I was back in the community where I grew up, different in everyone's eyes since I had been away for five years yet picked up from where we had left off. There were still some homes destroyed from the 1983 riots, and some homes had been rebuilt. Once a month, I would bring the fisherman brand new notes from the bank to exchange for their fishy-smelling currency notes. It was a ritual we had. I loved the exchange that continued to build the bonds in a community that was fighting against the politics of hate to heal itself, one human connection at a time.

The new branch team consisted of three of us in management ranks and remaining client-facing professionals. I was in the same age range as the client-facing team, and we were able to establish a committed working rigor alongside the ability to embrace lighthearted comradery. The long hours and arduous task of getting a startup off the ground required attention to detail, mindfulness of customer service, and accuracy as to not put anything money-related or regulatory in nature at risk. Nalaka, Viranga, Ruchira, Rizney, Ranga, and Thilak were the young men on the team, while Shra, Shehnai, Miranjala, and Shums were the ladies. Nihal, Milroy, and I had the honor of working with this great team to bring the branch to life and make sure it thrived.

Our days were long. One of the regulatory requirements on the island is that each bank had to balance the books in all currencies to report and settle the daily requirements with the central bank. This meant, if one branch of the bank was out of balance for one currency, even by a cent, we could not close the books. **The culture of the team was such that if one branch was out of balance, team members from the branches that were in balance would come over and help find the root cause of the problem and fix it so we could all go home.** Having been trained by the Kollupitaya branch team and now in the Wellawatta Branch operations, I had the relationships with all the young men who never hesitated to roll up their sleeves and get the job done. **There were never any recriminations. It was our team. It was our shared responsibility. We helped each other learn and grow.** This is a workplace culture I had assumed normal, but upon coming to the United States, I learned that it was not the case. However, I never forgot the joy and strength of such a fearlessly committed team and the power of success such a team brought to any organization.

I will never forget the early days, filled with system rollout issues, balancing glitches, and long hours of reconciliation that went into getting the operations started. Reconciling and verifying had to be done uninterrupted, and that meant sometimes those involved never got to stop for supper. We closed the bank for customers around 3:00 p.m. and then wrapped up our internal processes. For an emergency, we did take care of customers who needed help. We were so comfortable with each other under pressure; the team members who were not in the thick of reconciliation made sure everyone got to eat. If that meant to feed the working team members because they were focused on work, they were fed. It was like being in a family. Outside of the bank building, the country was in turmoil. Inside those four walls, we were family. We cared about each other, laughed, and held space for each other and their families.

I certainly learned quite a bit of life lessons from the young men on the team. For the first time in my life, I was around young men who were of different races and religions than mine and felt much at ease. I did not have to worry about open safety pins and chili powder. I did not have to worry about their intentions. They had my back—not just at work, but also in life. The ladies approached life a bit differently, but Shra, with her heart of gold and always ready to help those in need, made a huge impact on the team. She was one of those young women who did not publicize the good she does, but quietly shaped the environment she was in, balancing firmness and humor. It was good to have a strong, kind woman on the team, and it made my days richer. As a team, we worked like a well-oiled machine. From time to time, we had new hires who came in to be trained, and Nilma was one of those trainees who has remained close to us over the years, proving that developing others to build atop what we had accomplished was a noble act that keeps paying forward.

Ranga and Ruch did not come from the big city and did not have the privileges as the rest of the team members. Ruch was focused on playing cricket for the Sri Lankan team. He finished work and went to practice like a prayer each day. I would bring him good food from home, so he had a nutritious meal and built the stamina to pursue his passion. Ranga and Ruch also got to learn English with me. They were helping me by protecting me while I was helping them live their respective purpose.

I remember the day Ranga decided to buy a TV for the family. Ranga, Ruch, and I made plans on a Friday and drove my car to pick up his TV on Saturday. We took it to his home and installed it. Ranga lived in a one-room house with his mom, dad, two brothers, and a sister. Despite their circumstances, that family was rich in humanity. Ranga's mom had a heart of gold. That day, when she met me, she hugged me, called me her daughter, and welcomed me into her heart. I fell in love with Ranga's little sister Jeevanthi, who is to this day my Nangi (little sister). I enjoyed traditional Sinhala food, comprising of rice, coconut sambal, salted dry fish, and vegetables. Ranga's mom knew how a make a one-room house a welcoming palace for a stranger. That was the first of many days I spent with the family, and thus began a bond that has stood the test of civil war, racial strife, time, distance, and space. Through Ranga, I acquired a family. A family that embraced me as its own extension. To later watch Ranga build a big home for his parents, watch his siblings grow up and do well in life, and see how well he thrived as a banker in the Middle East, where his own son only speaks English, is a joyful success story. While his parents have since passed away, not an opportunity goes by without Nangi and me talking about the old days and the blessing her mom was to us both.

Ruchira (Ruch) came from Mathara, a beautiful southern coastal town. His family was equally kind and welcoming. Ruvini, his sister, became my sister, and I was introduced to his full extended family. I felt welcome by a large contingency of family members who made time for me and invested in building a meaningful relationship. Since his immediate family was far away, I made sure I looked out for Ruch, just as much as he looked out for me. Ruch made sure I was always safe, protected, and not in any risk. Even when I started taking night classes later on in my career, Ruch made sure I was not driving my car alone at night after 9:30 p.m. as a Tamil woman in a country that does not guarantee safety to minorities. He would take the bus and come to my school and drive me home and then take the bus home. He took the responsibility of being my protector seriously, and I would not have traded it for anything in the world! It was amazing to watch Ruch go on to play cricket for the Sri Lankan team as a bowler and then enter the world of international cricket umpiring. He never failed to give Ranga and me tickets for the game, and I always enjoyed the game. I have watched him marry and become a dad to two beautiful children. Our bond is strong after all these years. We not only stay in touch but make time to visit each other and make new memories with our families.

There were times when four to five young men walked me home and made sure my family was safe for the evening before going to their respective homes. My serious-minded traditional Tamil parents could not fathom any of this. **My mom lamented that people are wondering how Kasthuri had so**

many boyfriends who all came home together. I knew this was beyond their comprehension. How can young people of different races, religions, and genders be good friends and treat each other with the kind of love only family had for each other amidst a civil war? That was the question others had. To me, there was no explanation needed. These were my friends. They were helping me in my healing, and they were protecting me from the harm to which I was exposed. I was helping them in their careers. **It was an example of a win-win collaboration where everyone came out better than how we each went in. I was building back relationships and meaningful bonds after everything had been burned down. I was building it without bias, embracing the goodness of the soul that lived within each person, regardless of the outer trappings.** I did not feel there was a need to explain anything. If people could recognize it, they will understand; if they were incapable of recognizing it, no explanation would open their minds.

One morning, I took the bus to the bank since I was running late. As the officer, I had the keys to the bank safe and ATM with me while Milroy had the combination to ensure duel control of cash. There was a fellow passenger who appeared to be too close to me for comfort, and I had asked him to maintain his distance. When he would not listen and made physical contact, I acted viscerally without thinking. I realized I was approaching the bus stop to disembark, so I grabbed him by his shirt collar and yanked him out of the bus as I got out. I suppose that was such an unexpected move for a traditionally dressed young woman. I had the element of surprise on my side. The bank security came running, asking what happened, and I asked them to open the door and take the man in. Once in the bank, I had security lock the door. Ruch jumped over the bank counter and came right away to play his role of protector-in-chief. The team called the police. I was on a roll and did not stop to think how the rest of the team was processing the scene unfolding. I proceeded to go through the pockets of the man who tried to pick my purse because I needed to make sure he did not take any bank keys. The man was yelling at me in Sinhala and accusing me of stealing his money. I did take all his money and turned it over to the police, along with turning him over. **Fear was not an emotion I gave into. I had learned to channel any semblance of fear to effectively handle the situation and resolve the root cause that triggered the emotion. It was a survival skill that had kept me alive for years. This was no exception. Except I had sent my entire team into shock!** Since then, the team talks about how I dragged some guy off the bus, and it is one of the funny stories we laugh about. Humor allowed us to keep things in perspective.

I eventually got promoted out of the branch operations into international trade finance, where I got to work with corporate clients on their supply chain process and financing. Letters of credit, bonds, guarantees, etc., were all things I learned. In this role, I had another group of men on my team, this time older. My reputation for being a friendly, approachable, and organized professional helped me build new relationships. While the head of that department did not appreciate my power of influence over the team members, I enjoyed my work, learned from my team, and evolved to hold my own. My food was always a hit with my team, and the men who worked for me were teased as being voodooed into submission. Jokes aside, everything I know today about finance, banking, and international trade, I learned from these men. I was young. I was Tamil. I was a woman. That did not matter to them because they saw me for the person I was. **Once again, this new team helped me see the truth that fear, anger, and hate have no place in human relationships, and only when we transcend those can we build to last.**

While at the bank, I got admission to do my MBA in the United States. I was able to negotiate a three-month vacation for the summer since I had worked my time there, accumulating my vacations for a time like this. Not only did the British executive in charge give me that time off, but he also gave me a letter for the US consulate office, guaranteeing me a job in one of the bank locations upon graduation, assuring I would not be a burden to the US society. **He was letting me go and take flight toward my lasting freedom, guaranteeing me a failsafe. The corporate world could be one with heart and humanity if the tone is set with intent at the top.** It was this letter that allowed me to get my US student visa, at a time when the US government had Sri Lankan Tamils classified as terrorists.

The bank also allowed me to convert what was left of my life savings at the bank rate, so I had maximum US dollars on me when I entered the United States. My friend Viranga purchased my car, so I did not have to look for a buyer in the open market, a car Ruch had helped me by a few years back. The goodness of this amazing team of bankers did not stop there. They gave me a four-leaf clover diamond pendant as a good luck gift on my last day so their well-wishes could see me through the challenges that lay ahead. **Where in the world would a group of union workers care enough about their management team member to do something that special? Where in the world, in spite of a civil war, would people have the courage to value the goodness of humanity above all else? Only in my beautiful Mother Lanka, where people have the courage and humanity to live their truth with the firm belief of politics and conservatism be damned!** My adopted home, the United States of America, would benefit from taking a page out of Sri Lanka's social contract that continues to help a small island nation thrive through the soul of its people.

It was with a heavy heart that I left both the bank and Sri Lanka. I was leaving my good friends behind. This time around, I had grown close to some of them. I cared deeply for them. These were my real relationships in Sri Lanka. The ones that would matter years from now because they were built on our shared humanity and not dictated by what was acceptable, given the ethnic strife and my family's conservative rules. **I knew I was leaving behind something rare and priceless. It was my hope that time and distance would not diminish what had been built. This had been more than a**

start to a career. It was the coming of age of a young professional woman stepping into a man's world with the support of the good men capable of overcoming biases to help her take her flight.

My experience with building teams and creating the psychological safety to bring out the best in each team member, without biases, was the single most important capability that propelled me to becoming a young female CFO within a unit of a large US conglomerate. I did have the skills and the know-how to navigate the FinTech disruption from my journey, and the second round in Sri Lanka gave me the finishing touch needed to shape my destiny. My career trajectory is living proof that the being leads the way so that the doing can drive sustainable organizational change. Without the strength of the being, the doing will become mere busywork.

It is so rare that people accept another for who they really are and give them the tools to succeed. I had all my team members teach me and help me become the professional I am today. We all learned something from each other. We all transformed each other's lives. My career happened because of the people on my teams and the trust that sustained us through difficult strategic decisions. My teams at the bank taught me to succeed together. That leg of my journey was the proof I need to affirm my theory of shared prosperity. Today, I firmly embrace shared prosperity in my graduate school teaching and strategic business consulting work. It helps me craft win-win solutions with the mindfulness needed to build fearless teams capable of innovation and growth. **I am a firm believer in people being our single most valuable resource. We succeed because of our people. Leading a team is both an honor and a sacred duty that cannot be taken lightly.**

Lessons Learned:

➢ *Leadership involves willingness to learn from the team and expand one's perspective.* Being able to transform others while being open to transforming ourselves in the process is the secret sauce for leading through authentic relationship-building.

➢ *One never knows how many lives are impacted by a business decision.* Being conscious of this fact is not optional for a leader because followers will lose faith and trust in a leader who is incapable of such compassion to understand the very fabric of humanity.

➢ *Continually checking our biases and actively working to overcome them is a necessary path to living a successful life of purpose.* It is when we open our hearts and minds that we let in the light, creativity, and collaboration. That is when lasting growth happens.

CHAPTER 10

LEARNING TO TRUST

"Just when the caterpillar thought the world was over, it became a butterfly."
—English Proverb

Eddie Murphy's "Coming to America" was playing in my head as I landed at the tiny airport in Terre Haute, Indiana. I had travelers' cheques in my purse, twenty pounds of luggage comprising of my clothes and books, along with my passport and graduate school paperwork—no cell phone. No cash. **I did not know a soul here, but I had arrived. I had hope. I had faith. I had a grateful heart filled with caring wishes.**

My new graduate housing roommate, a second-year student, was supposed to pick me up at the airport, per the university communication. Given the size of the airport, my luggage was put on the curbside, and the airport shutdown upon landing. It was the last flight, and they were closed for business. I had been traveling for hours, from Colombo via Dubai, London, and Houston, into Terre Haute, living through a never-ending day as I gained time traveling west. My body clock was in the next day already. Dusk slowly turned into a dark night. The airport road was empty, with no activity. I sat on my luggage, wondering if my new roommate would ever show up or if the university would notice I had not arrived and make alternate arrangements to pick me up. I did not have access to a phone, had no directional guidance, and had no way to get to my destination. Waiting patiently was my only option, and I kept singing my heart out to keep myself awake. Falling asleep was not an option.

Just past midnight, a car filled with Indiana students pulled up, and my new roommate apologetically explained how she had forgotten to pick me up. I quietly put my luggage in the trunk and got in the car. I did not see the point in engaging in a discussion other than greeting them. Responsible individuals never leave people stranded, and I had the feeling that I needed to stay on guard. Luckily, the graduate housing was much closer to the airport than the university itself. I got out in the parking lot and got my luggage out of the car. The Indiana students drove off to the party they were at prior to picking me up. I did not mind because I needed to be alone and settle in. As I tried carrying everything up a few steps to the lift, an American gentleman walked in and said, "Hi, I am Mike Henry. Let me help you." I introduced myself and thanked him for the help, assuming he was the warden of the graduate housing. He started explaining to me that he was at a party and apologized for having had a few beers. I thought to myself, *how respectful of him to do so, especially when I had just left a country where men drank an entire bottle of coconut whiskey for lunch and carried on with business as usual.* This was the precursor to all that was new in life yet to unfold. I smiled and said good night as I reached the third floor. Mike helped me get my luggage to my apartment door and bid goodnight.

I took the weekend to settle in and prepared to explore the university campus as Monday came around. I had a leisurely thirty-minute walk to campus from graduate housing. The summer was hot but dry, and I was ready to take on my day all dressed in cotton and walking shoes. I had arrived a week early to get my bearings and be prepared for summer classes. **While it is normal for students to start university in spring or fall semesters, I only had the money for the shorter summer semester, and I decided to make my own path to suit my pocketbook. Nothing about my life thus far had been normal; therefore, normal for me was being purposeful in my choices rooted in my reality.** I had two overarching goals for the week before classes started. One was to meet my school of business dean, as well as faculty, to establish a relationship. Two was to figure out how to get a graduate assistantship that would pay for the education and give me a living stipend.

The walk to campus was rather interesting. I had never been to a country where people drove on the other side of the road, and even the cars had the driver's seat in the opposite place than I was used to. Life seemed to happen in a mirror image in the United States. Even the light switches worked upside down. I made a mental note to myself to observe what others were doing before doing things based on habit and instinct. I needed to adjust and reorient to assimilate and integrate into the society I found myself in. The curiosity got the better of me, and I embraced the experience with a steady sense of humor and awe. Keeping the inner child in me alive at twenty-seven was going to come in handy!

I also noticed that there were no roundabouts. Instead, there were stop signs. Drivers were stopping and waiting, even when there were no pedestrians to cross the street. This was remarkably interesting to me. I thought to myself, *what a waste of petrol and time.* As I kept walking, I decided to cut through parking lots and entertain myself by exploring the exterior of the buildings I passed by. As I came upon an elementary school, my curiosity totally got the better of me. So, I walked up to the window facing the parking lot and peeked in. What caught my attention was the words posted on the drop-ceiling surface for only the teacher to read from her position, which faced the students. **The message to the teacher was, "Who you are speaks so loud that the children are not hearing a word of what you say." What an important reminder to all teachers, and adults, for that matter. It resonated with me and made me feel happy that I was in a country that understood the importance of being an authentic being, so what we were doing had an impact.** It was a few months before I realized the messages posted are to remind folks to adhere to principles and are not always emblematic of what folks naturally embodied.

I walked up to the business school and took the lift to the top floor to meet with the dean. I had an appointment, and I had arrived a bit early. I took the opportunity to greet and get to know the administrative team since they were all going to be a part of my life for the next two years of the MBA program. The meeting with the dean went well, but he could not help me with a graduate assistantship. He recommended that I apply for a summer student job on campus for minimum wage, $4.25/hour. I was appreciative of any insight and opportunity presented to me. I did not have a winning hand, and I had to play the cards I held. I was happy and hopeful that I could find something. Armed with a university map, I said my goodbyes and tried to leave, but for the life of me, I could not find the lift. I asked the administrative team for the lift, and they said they were busy, which made no sense to me. Instead of bothering them, I walked around, asking others. Finally, Keith, a second-year graduate student, advised me to use the term "elevator" and showed me to the elevator banks that were hidden behind the vending machines. I chatted with Keith for a bit and bid farewell.

I walked all through campus, applying for jobs and meeting with deans to look for any opportunity. My approach was to get to know them while I gave them an opportunity to get to know me. Once I understood what their team did, I made an offer of how I could be of service. All departments hired their own students, which meant if the business school had nothing for me, no one else would give me a job because they had to employ students majoring in the field of that department. I stopped at the student commons for lunch and to regroup. The water fountain at the entrance was soothing, and the opportunity to sit down and relax was wonderful. I went through the campus map one more time, but this time used the index list of departments. It occurred to me that I should identify university departments that did not pertain to any field of study and then target them. That way, I could pragmatically simplify my job search. Pleased with this sudden burst of insight, I opened my bank account to deposit all my travelers' cheques, withdrew one hundred dollars, and searched for something to eat. Fast food and processed drinks were never my thing. I had grown up with natural, organic products and nothing looked appetizing to me. I was happy to find out there was a Chinese restaurant in the commons that would make me noodles or fried rice with the ingredients of my choice. Beef and broccoli with hot chili spice were what I decided to try. Spicy lunch with hot green tea, and the world felt all right to me.

The last department I stopped by for the day was continuing education. Dean Jensen and his team were welcoming. They normally never have students like me walk in to get to know them or look for a job. That was music to my ears. There was hope, and I was the queen of hope! I decided to get to know the four administrative ladies working for the department. Michelle, Vicky, Earlene, and Judy were lovely older ladies who were using typewriters and three-ply paper to do their work. As I chatted with them, I observed the piles of unfiled documents, manual processing, and typing going on. It surprised me that this is how 1995 looked like in the US when even Sri Lanka had progressed far beyond that era. **Judging was not my role here, but using my judgment to pragmatically negotiate something was.** I asked them if they would like help around the office and shared with them ways in which I could make their life better. By now, Earlene was having a stiff neck sitting and typing all day. Watching her in pain bothered me, and I offered to relieve her pain. They were surprised and asked what I would do to make the pain go away. I explained to them that I was used to giving my mom massages and my healing hands had the ability to remove stress knots and pain.

This small, impromptu, informal chat session while they worked was turning into an interesting situation, and they were all curious to see how I was going to relieve Earlene of her pain. I asked if any of them had lotion, and they gave me some lavender lotion. I used the lotion to gently massage Earlene's neck, and as I worked the stress knot, she got so relaxed that she fell asleep. My kindness and ability to help a person in pain made me a hit with the ladies. Michelle immediately walked into Dean Jensen's office and told him that she was hiring me to help the team with filing, shredding, and any other work they needed. It was noticeably clear Michelle was in charge, and she ran the department. I had the job, and we were all happy. The unspoken arrangement was that they had a student masseuse at their service, and I was okay with that. This was the start of a wonderful lifelong relationship with four amazing women, and I no longer felt alone or isolated.

When I narrated this story to others in graduate housing, they asked me, "Why did you go from being a banker to shredding and filing? Isn't it going to look awful on your resume?" I just smiled and said nothing. I knew the opportunity that presented itself because filing and shredding involved documents, and I would have access to a wealth of information. It was up to me to make that opportunity count. I also had forged a relationship with four women who were going to be my allies. This was not about a resume. This was about building to last, and I was building my destiny. I did not need others to understand it. Over the summer, I learned everything I needed to know. This department ran the entire summer semester for the university, including payroll. They also ran the state of Indiana prison education programs, Ivy Tech Community College Distance education, as well as high school summer honors to introduce students to the university education.

I started building Excel spreadsheets to automate the financial processes, applying my banking and technology experience. I trained the ladies to use the basic prototype and showed them what else I could do. As I built and showed them a simplified, automated way to manage their processes more efficiently, they kept telling Dean Jensen how awesome Kas was and the magic she was creating in the office. As we approached the end of the summer semester, I approached Dean Jensen and proposed to him that I fully automate his department's financial processes and train his team to manage it, so it is sustainable long past my graduation. In return, he would create a graduate assistantship for me and pick up my full tuition and give me a living stipend. **The dean was getting a six-figure value, and Michelle had already done the gardening on my behalf. So, we shook hands and made the deal. The shredding and filing summer job had transformed into a full-ride to an MBA program.**

Dr. Bialaszewski was my first professor on campus, and he was rather unconventional. This suited me greatly, and he made an extra effort to help me get oriented with how things worked in the US. We built a good student-professor relationship that sustained me over the two years, and upon graduation, we have remained friends exchanging ideas and celebrating successes. Most business school professors were rather detached, but Dr. B was a welcome change from my perspective. Students were highly competitive with each other, and even team projects were not collaborative since everyone searched for an edge over the others. It was a good introduction to what the business world held for me and what I needed to be prepared for as I entered the world of work in the US.

Alongside the graduate assistantship, I was able to secure a research assistant job at the science library. I worked on the weekends, a schedule that was impossible to fill as all students focused the weekends on attending to their families or enjoying life. I had neither option at my disposal as one of the few single individuals in graduate housing. I rented a piece of gardening space from the housing department to grow herbs and summer vegetables. I paid, in tomatoes and cucumbers, the student whose apartment faced my plot to guard my vegetables. I made friends with graduate students who had kids, so I had the opportunity for some play. **Life was falling into place, and I was emerging as a constant gardener. A gardener of relationships. A gardener of win-win negotiations. A gardener of my own solutions.**

The housing was a four-apartment complex grouping on the banks of the Wabash River. Each apartment building fanned into three wings, with the elevator shaft forming the central core, and each wing had four floors. The buildings were in the four corners surrounding a central housing complex park, playground, and BBQ pavilion with picnic benches. It was a rather open and inviting set up with the opportunity for everyone to enjoy the outdoors. That summer, an older Indian woman befriended me in graduate housing. Her name was Vasantha, and she spoke Tamil. She was getting a sociology master's and was having a challenging time adjusting to the US culture. She needed my help with various things, and I was happy to help a fellow student. I had someone to talk in Tamil, and that was a welcomed opportunity to remain connected to my roots.

I sat talking to Vasantha one Saturday evening as her new Malaysian roommate, Marina, moved in. Helping Marina move was Mike, the same gentleman who had helped me a couple of weeks back. We all helped Marina get her belongings into her room and sat in the living room/kitchen shared space to chat with each other. The impromptu international gathering of graduate students was an unexpected treat, and we all enjoyed the interaction. Vasantha enjoyed the conversation so much that she insisted that we all meet up every Sunday with a dish of our choice to share. Mike suggested we all then walk into town to the two-dollar movies at the historic theater. That evening, a social engagement group was formed, and the apartment Vasantha and Marina shared was to be our gathering place. That evening, I learned that Mike was a graduate student and not the warden, as I had assumed. Thus, began our Sunday gatherings that kept growing in size and food variety.

Over time, Mike and I had become friends and enjoyed our philosophical discussions that delved into history, politics, and world religions. As students, we needed to be careful with our spending, and our gatherings helped us plan our meals and coordinate grocery shopping. It was prudent for us to shop together and then split the cost and quantities of groceries to stretch our dollars. When it came to dry goods, we gathered more friends and shopped at the local Sam's Club, splitting everything five ways. We were mastering frugality with win-win strategies. The bonus was that I always had friends with cars to get a ride. One Friday evening, we had just returned from Sam's Club and started portioning out the groceries in my apartment when my father called me from Sri Lanka. The other friends left with their share of the purchases, while Mike stayed back to settle-up with me. I figured he would not understand the conversation in Tamil anyway, and there was no harm.

My father never calls me, and I was concerned that something terrible had happened at home. However, when I learned his intent, I was heartbroken. My father proceeded to tell me that *I cannot be out there in the western world without getting married. With my independent streak and bold nature, no young man would want to marry me. He had found a widower who was much older than me with three children, and I should feel lucky that someone was willing to marry me. I would have a steady hand to give me structure and family by agreeing to this marriage.* I calmly told my father to go to hell and stay there. Then I hung up on him. I let my emotions get the better of me, and for the first time in years, sobbed my heart out. I had forgotten Mike was in the apartment, waiting in the kitchen to settle-up the groceries.

My sobbing must have scared the daylights out of Mike, for he knocked on my room door and asked if everything was okay. My roommate was in her room, finishing up her week's projects. I took a few minutes to settle myself and came out. The understanding, kindness, and compassion with which Mike proceeded to inquire what had happened made me cry all over again. I was a guarded person behind my open, friendly persona. This was a totally unguarded moment. I explained to him the conversation that had taken place without even thinking that it would sound like utter nonsense to an American who had no concept of arranged marriages. He was so livid that a father would talk to a daughter that way, he wanted to call my father and lecture him on how to be a dad. Well, that was not going to happen. I was in the US, and nothing could happen to me that I did not want. And knowing that was my strength. From that day onward, Mike took extra care in making sure I did not feel sad or isolated.

Working on the graduate assistantship during the day, attending my MBA classes at night, and working at the science library on the weekends kept me busy, and all the free time I had was spent on projects, assignments, and planning for my job search. My faculty advised me that I should lower my expectations, especially with a name like mine; no one would even call me for an interview. Saying things like that to me is akin to waving a red cloth in front of a bull. My determination only multiplied. Officially, my name was Vadivambikai Kasthuri Gulasingam. It did not fit in the Social Security system or the university system. I was told names were not supposed to be that long. No one cared about the fact that Gulasingam was not my surname; it was my father's first name. We do not have surnames because no one is another person's property. We are each our own person with our own name. Mike helped me strategize the resume writing and recommended that I use the initial of my first name and just proceed with showcasing what I brought to the table.

The fall semester turned to the spring semester, and I got to experience my first winter. I was not happy when the temperature dipped below seventy degrees. I had no idea how the snow season would feel. I was utterly ill-prepared. Once again, Mike came to my rescue and took me to the local thrift store so I could buy winter clothes and shoes. **I had never heard of used clothing stores but was grateful to have the right clothes at a price I could afford. Now, when I donate to the thrift store every year, I do it with a heartfelt appreciation for the kindness of strangers who kept me warm during cold hard winters.**

One ordinary day, the Asian students in the graduate housing were advised that the ingredients we were using to cook were stinking up the surrounding area. The situation did not end there, and it turned unbearable for us. We knew the town we were in was not an enlightened one; it was in West Central Indiana, a state that was not known for its racial diversity or tolerance. The American students who had enjoyed all the culinary delights were equally offended by what was going on. Under Mike's leadership, all the outrage against the intolerance was channeled into forming a student organization to stage a peaceful protest. Mike came up with the name, "Student Coalition for Administrative Reform" (SCAR). He and I partnered to develop a signature campaign to get as many students as possible to sign on. **It was the start of our peaceful protest: international students and US students, side by side, united in the demand for tolerance and justice.** Having worked for the student newspaper, he knew how to work the system, and the letter with all the signatures was published, highlighting what was wrong about the situation at hand. Faculty from various departments rallied around the students to voice their concerns, but the business school chose to stay out of it.

What started as an initial press release turned into university radio and newspaper debates with those siding with the administration against the international students from Asia on one side and the rest of the university on the other side. I was directly impacted by this as an Asian student, and I was one of the few who were articulate enough in English to take on the issue in the media. We were told that all policy changes need to come up via the student government, and graduate students had no right to participate in student government; it was the purview of undergraduate students. We may not be able to have representation, but we could organize and run a diverse slate of candidates to influence policy changes. Being the political science graduate student, Mike was on the ball with getting things organized. By now, I was the unpaid statistics tutor for his full class, which made the political science graduate class, our ally. **We had an official platform, candidates, and targeted campaign. Our slate won, and we started guiding some changes.**

None of this was going to solve the underlying issues, and we knew it. Mike's former girlfriend worked for the outside press, and she offered to give him and me the opportunity to make our case to the community that coming Monday. On Sunday evening, the president of the university called Mike in his apartment and summoned him and the foreign student, me, to the office for an early-morning meeting. **It appeared that the outside press had called him to ask for his side of the story, and that was the straw that broke the proverbial camel's back. It forced the university president to do something.**

Monday morning, Mike, Matt (another political scient graduate student), and I went to the office of the university president. In attendance was the entire senior administration. The meeting started, and each of the two US students got to share their perspectives on the injustice afoot. When it came to my turn, the president leaned back in his chair and shut his eyes as if he needed to take a relaxing nap. It was that red cloth waving, once again, that ignites my energy to act with purpose and precision. *In a calm, quiet voice, I addressed the president and said, "I come from a culture that washes with soap and water every time we go to the bathroom. You, sir, on the other hand, come from a culture that uses paper. Have we ever walked up to you and told you that you stink like a mobile outhouse?"*

The president shot straight up on his chair and asked, "You talking to me?" Well, I got what I needed. I had his full attention, and he was channeling his inner Robert DeNiro. This was progress. I responded, "Yes, sir, I am talking to you. If you are so offended with the smell of food as it is prepared to be eaten, how offensive do you think it is when it exits the human body? If we are happy to pay our tuition with a premium and adjust to your norms, what gives you the right to deny us the ability to occupy the space for which we have paid rent? Why can we not eat what is healthy? Why should we be forced to adopt unhealthy eating habits?" I had not only shocked the entire administration; I had shocked Mike and Matt. Everyone stared at me, and there was pin-drop silence in the room. I had made my point, and no one knew how to respond to me. No one had expected the foreign student to have a mic-drop moment.

When we got out of there, Mike and I headed toward the department of continuing education. We got a standing ovation from folks around campus cheering us on. We had no idea why they were cheering because we did not realize that what happened behind closed doors would travel that fast across campus. When we got to my continuing education team, it was Earlene who gave us a high-five and told me she was so proud of us for having the guts to stand up the powers of the university. Mike and I became known as a formidable team, and I became the foreign student who called the university president *a mobile outhouse.* **I had a graduate assistantship that paid for my education, I handled the university financial process, and I had taken on the power structure with Mike by my side. If they took the assistantship from me, my visa would get revoked, and I would be back in the civil war. But I made a conscious choice to speak truth to power, stand up with dignity in my truth, and be my authentic self.** I had Mike and the majority of the faculty and students behind me. **We decided not to hand over our power to a handful of individuals. Instead, we took our power, and together, demanded dignity for all.** Long story short, most of the administrators were removed from their positions, and the president became a simple faculty member. There was a meaningful change on campus. A new era had dawned, and we had made it happen.

Through this first year journey in graduate school, I had not only earned a good friend, but I was also learning to trust. It is not every day that I have the honor of someone taking on my battle as theirs and put themselves at risk. Mike did that for me to fight for my dignity. Through him, all his professors, classmates, and friends became the firewall to take down a system of injustice. For the first time in my life, I had a best friend who would fight my battles without reservation. He asked for nothing in return. It was a pure friendship of the most meaningful kind.

The universe was helping me heal by presenting the opportunity to lose the final baggage I was holding on to—lack of trust. Trust was not something that was going to come easy after the life I had. Yet, the recent events were transforming me. I was beginning to see unconditional kindness and friendship taken to this ultimate extent, where everything he was working toward could be taken away from him because he stood up to fight my fight. Ironically, I had my own archangel who lived up to the purpose of his name, Michael. He led the charge to slay my dragons and taught me that I could start trusting. **Mike was clearing the final hurdle I had in front of me to free my soul so I could fully embrace my purpose as a whole person. With my heart, mind, body, and soul, piece by piece, he helped put me back together, after earning my trust and giving me the opportunity to be openly vulnerable for the expressed purpose of my final transformation. I was finally becoming a butterfly.**

My ability to be vulnerable and hold space for others would not be possible today had I not had the opportunity to learn to trust. As awful and offensive as it was, what was done to others and me on campus presented the opportunity for my much-needed transformation. It is always our trials and tribulations that polish us to sparkle. It was also a good reminder that just because **I had walked away from the civil war does not mean I am free of racial and ethnic injustice. This understanding has helped shape my professional and personal life in the present-day United States of America, where I am continually reminded that I do not belong here. I am the other. I am an alien.** I realize that deep-seated fear causes people to oppress those they believe to be the "other." I take every opportunity to demonstrate that I am just as human with the same inalienable rights. When that fails, I am extremely comfortable inviting folks to see my alien craft hidden away in my garage. A bit of humor never hurt, right? When I am told to go back to where I came from, I smile and remind them that they should get a head start since their folks came by boat, and they have a long journey ahead. Since I flew in, I had time to fly back.

Workplaces are no different from the university. There are always the snide remarks that turn into an environment of harassment. Microaggression is commonplace. Learning to separate the noise and keeping the focus is paramount. **The intent of the biases is to alienate and diminish the value of those of us who are perceived to be different. Our task is not to play into their hands and embrace victimhood.** I deny everyone the ability to get into my head and manipulate me. I decide what I give permission to in my life. Sometimes, the aggressors have the audacity to ask me why I do not get upset or quit, and I gently remind them that **how they treat me is a reflection of their own station in life. How I treat them with dignity in spite of their behavior reflects my station in life.** Sometimes I even advise them to read *Hamlet*, my favorite play of Shakespeare, so they get some much-needed perspective from western literature.

It is now twenty-five years after I first met Mike in the elevator of graduate housing. We have been happily married for twenty-two years, sharing a fulfilling life, and living our purpose. We have never stopped trusting or caring, and knowing we have each other has given us the strength to take life on with courage. A Tamil proverb loosely translated in English states, "*Your teacher and your spouse shape your destiny.*" Sr. Julia and Mike have surely shaped mine! **The gratitude that fills my heart has enough positive brain chemistry to keep me happy, content, and purposeful that nothing takes me off my game. I have my true north to anchor me.**

Today, as a member of Warren Buffet's Duracell team, I have the honor of hearing his wisdom. **The key to success, as Warren Buffet describes, is "choosing the person you marry"** (https://www.cnbc.com/2018/02/14/warren-buffett-this-partnership-will-determine-your-success.html). **I wholeheartedly agree with him. I have both my best friend and husband rolled into one person. Having that kind of trust, unconditional love, and unwavering acceptance anchors the soul while allowing me to soar high in the direction of my purpose.** I see so many leaders and talented individuals not fulfill their potential or live their purpose because they do not have the anchor to ground them. That is harmful to both the confidence and the ability to be vulnerable. Without the ability to have confidence and vulnerability, one can never lead. Insecurity takes over, and negative toxic energy surrounds such situations, preventing collaboration, innovation, and growth.

LESSONS LEARNED:

> ➤ ***Learning to trust is fundamental to living life with purpose.*** Trusting empowers us to show our vulnerability. Trusting allows us to take flight in the direction of our dreams, knowing we are anchored to a meaningful life—the ability to trust shapes our leadership journey to be the change.

> ➤ ***Giving in to the biases of others and allowing their single twisted perspective to become our story must be faced head-on with unwavering courage.*** Our relationships give us the strength to stand up to oppression and intimidation intended to get us off our game. Being a constant gardener of relationships is the ultimate superpower that could bring corrupt power to its knees.

> ➤ ***The only family we get to choose in this life is our spouse, so choose wisely.*** Who you marry determines your success because it shapes your psyche and influences your ability to be in the moment and embrace vulnerability with confidence. Knowing you are loved unconditionally and supported as you are is the undiluted high needed to thrive without reserve.

CHAPTER 11

RISING ABOVE

During my second year in the MBA program, I started interviewing for jobs and building a professional network. While I had to start from scratch in the US, I drew from my professional life from overseas and leaned into my new university network. Everyone knew someone, and every relationship had the potential to become something meaningful. I tirelessly cultivated, weeded, and gardened. I looked at it as an investment as opposed to a task. I also decided to convert my banking experience and professional credentials into something of value in the US.

My research informed me that the Association of Financial Professionals (AFP) certified treasury professionals, and the content of the qualifications was a subset of what I had earned for my banking. In addition, it was clear that my banking experience qualified me to apply for full professional credentialing, as opposed to the associate role students with no experience were given. Dr. John Zietlow, in our finance department, was the author of the book used to prepare students and professionals to sit for the exam, and I had the opportunity to take that course as an elective within my finance specialization. I could kill two birds with one stone: get my MBA specialization credit, and prepare to sit for the Certified Treasury Professional (CTP) credentialing exam. Once the decision was made, I met with Dr. Zietlow and planned with him. A spiritual man at the core, he not only was supportive of my decision, but he also encouraged me to sit for the exam right after completing the course.

I successfully completed the course and passed the credentialing exam in my first sitting. I was accepted as a full CTP even before completing my MBA. Now, I had a way to showcase my international experience as authenticated by the US professional credential. The credential also enabled me to become a member of AFP and join any local chapter I wanted. I leveraged the decision to join a local chapter as a *manna from heaven* for networking. I started getting to know corporate treasurers in the major cities, but Chicago was close to where I was and the local chapter, Treasury Management Association of Chicago (TMAC), was extremely welcoming of me. Banks and pharmaceutical firms were interested in my experience, but banks could not hire a foreign student due to work visa restrictions. I kept casting a wider net and applying for jobs as they appeared in the newspaper and online job boards. Every time I had an interview, Mike would drive me to the city I needed to be. Cincinnati, Cleveland, Columbus, Indianapolis, St. Louis, and Chicago were regular destinations, and we were able to drive back and forth on the same day to keep costs low.

The relentless effort paid off when I was called in for an interview with TCI, the Denver-based telecom company that served the Chicago market, encompassing Indiana, Illinois, and Wisconsin. They flew me into Chicago for the interview and put me up in a hotel. The full three-part interview with HR, the hiring manager, and the VP of the operation all took place on the same day. Steve White, the VP of the Chicago operations, was direct, tough, but also principled. He hid his compassionate side well, but with a bit of humor-filled probing, we found that we were kindred spirits—tough on the outside, yet kind and compassionate on the inside. Steve had only one concern, and that was he could not verify any of my banking references since they were foreign. He was direct in asking me if he could trust me and take the chance.

Directness is a trait I value, and I can handle it. I said, "Steve if you make a mistake in hiring me, you will only lose the days I am employed before you can remedy the situation by firing me. On the other hand, if I made a mistake, I will be back in my home country in the civil war, and my life itself could be lost. So, I have everything to lose in this situation. I am a person of my word. When I give you my word, I give you my honor. I will fulfill my duties to prove to you that you made the right decision. And when I do that, I need for you to give me your word that you will sponsor my work permit and help me stay in the US because once this one-year practical training is over, I need an employer sponsorship to remain in the US."

On the open and honest discussion of two adult professionals and a handshake, that deal was sealed, and I had myself a job in Chicago one month prior to graduating with my MBA. Steve shared his family background with me; we both understood that our circumstances do not define us.

I needed to start work in Chicago as soon as I cleared the drug test. That meant my practical training paperwork had to be approved and delivered to me. I had less than a week to accomplish all this and make arrangements with my professors to wrap up my projects early and complete my MBA

remotely in the last two weeks. Having meaningful relationships with faculty and administrative personnel proved to be
a blessing. My paperwork was couriered to Washington, DC,
signed, and returned to me in forty-eight hours, thanks to Dr.
Robert Clouse. Dr. Close was a renowned history professor
who not only became my extended family on campus but also
officiated our wedding when Mike and I got married at the
university chapel a year later.

My career in the US started with telecommunication in
1997, alongside the deregulation of the industry. This resulted
in the merging of voice, video, and data, giving way to a wave
of mergers and acquisitions. I got my M&A operational experience working through the integration of newly acquired
telecom providers and eventually work through the acquisition of TCI by AT&T Broadband. Through it all, as I grew in my
career and supported Steve's strategic vision for the organization, he kept his word and sponsored me for my green card.
I got incredibly challenging finance and business operations
assignments, and every time I delivered results, he kept his
end of the bargain.

By now, Mike had proposed to me about five times, and I
had moved from a firm "no" the first time to, "Yes, but I will
not marry you until I apply for my paperwork through my
employer." Friendship is important to me, and Mike was my
best friend. I had never thought about marriage, and in the
US, marriages did not last. I explained to him that I could
not sacrifice a life-long relationship with my best friend
for a transient US marriage. He understood my reasoning
but remained persistent. He also respected my stance on
no dating because I did not come from a dating culture,
hence his persistent proposals. Within a year of working in
Chicago, I had applied for my employer sponsorship, and
I married Mike in Terre Haute, Indiana, at the university
chapel. The entire arrangement was coordinated by the
Department of Continuing Education and the professors
who had supported us as students.

Dr. Glenn Perry, the renowned political science scholar, gave me away; Dr. David Johnson, Mike's academic advisor, gave his Victorian home for the reception; Dr. Robert Clouse officiated the wedding since he was also an ordained minister. Dr. Bonadelle Clouse played the wedding march as Dr. Perry walked me down the aisle. Judy, Earlene, and the team from continuing education booked the hotel suite for us and coordinated all the arrangements. It was a university reunion. The wedding cake came from the local Walmart. I wore a white silk saree purchased in Chicago and made my own blouse. The wedding bouquet was put together by me with pink and white carnations and baby's breath. It was simple, intimate, and had in attendance my AT&T teammates and our university family. Everyone decided they liked my Sri Lankan food. So, I cooked and went to church to get married. The serving and cleaning up was done by our friends. It was a unique experience that did not cost us even a thousand dollars, but we were happy and felt rich with blessings for the people we had in our lives.

The wedding was held on the last weekend in June, and Sunday night, Mike and I moved to Chicago. I was back at work on Monday. Life was falling into place. I had a job that I loved and worked for someone who valued me. I had my best friend as my husband, a situation I had never envisioned. We were settling into a routine. As the industry consolidation happened, telecom giants were swapping territories to consolidate market power. All AT&T assets in the Chicagoland area were being sold to Comcast, and the AT&T brand was sold to SBC Ameritech. All the industry trends that led to all this is for another time and another place because it is definitely worth exploring. However, what is important to note here is that **when organizations do not innovate and grow with the changing times, they self-select to become obsolete. I had a front-row seat to that steady march within the industry. It also became a wake-up call to make sure I am always current and relevant so as not to become obsolete myself.**

One of the conscious choices I made upon moving to Chicago was joining the local treasury organization as well as being present at the local and national conferences. My next job was not going to be based on newspaper advertisements. It was going to come via my professional network. I worked through my final transition at AT&T and had a year before I had my green card in my hand. Meanwhile, I had a valid work permit that required me to maintain a job of a certain title and compensation to remain a part of the work visa process. I landed in a mining and manufacturing HQ operations in the Chicago market. Just when I received my green card, I was hired by AON for their risk management division. This is where I first became a CFO in my early thirties. The experience at AON was much like my first job at the bank. There was a close-knit culture, and the entrepreneurial spirit of innovation was valued. Creative ideas were supported and rewarded. What started as the financial business partner to restructure the organization and establish robust financial processes with integrated predictive analytics evolved into a regional structure and the offer to become the regional CFO.

I had led the initiative for financial process automation, building from the ground up a business intelligence system with a data warehouse to help agile analytics-based decisions support. I loved the opportunity to combine my technology skills and my financial capabilities. My age, gender, or nationality was not an issue in this organization, and I was given the opportunity to thrive. I built my own team, developed them, and also collaborated with the holding company to establish an early career development program to have a reliable recruiting pipeline integrated with employee career development and the organization's succession plan for business continuity. By now, I was teaching for two universities as a visiting professor, and I was able to bring the work of learning and working together.

During my tenure at AON, 9/11 happened. Our New York office was in Tower 2, and the data backup was in Tower 1. Our global headquarters was in Chicago, right across Millennium

Park by Lake Michigan. I ended up in Green Bay, Wisconsin, due to flights being rerouted that morning. My boss was in New York. **I was patched into a live video conference from our Green Bay office just before the second tower was hit. It was like being in Sri Lanka all over again. Who got hurt, who will live, how do we notify family, and so much more were running through my mind. I immediately drove back to Chicago, and we started strategizing for disaster recovery. This was not a normal course of business. This was business in a warzone.** Every plane that went down that day was owned by an airline company that was our client. We had not just lost our New York office; our clients had sustained massive losses, and we had to take care of business while trying to take care of our own. Calls were coming in from the rubble, begging us to send first responders to specific locations before they ran out of air to breathe.

Most senior leaders and staff could not handle the emotional trauma of the moment that stretched into days. Coming from a war-ravaged island, I had the ability to channel my emotions into action. I worked with the leadership team to identify fellow team members with similar backgrounds so we could take calls from families looking for their loved ones and manage through the human moments. I will never forget the three-hundred-plus employees and clients we lost that day. We had a new hire on their first day and calling the family to give the news was one of the hardest things we had ever done. The heroism of people who stayed back to help others run to safety; senior leaders who ran into the building to get the teams out; the executive assistant who stayed back to secure the data and document work were all some of the realities that will stay in my heart for as long as I shall live.

We worked our role and performed disaster recovery for New York. We had to take care of all the clients. This was not the time to feel sad, sorry, or cry. Our teams worked tirelessly, and the spouses understood the extraordinary circumstances. Our lives changed in one instant. It was also a time when our humanity came through. Just a few months ago, when we realized our office cleaning lady was pregnant, my team organized a baby shower for her. We wanted her to feel a part of our team and celebrated her pregnancy, just like we would one of our team members. The entire cleaning crew was touched by our gesture, and we were simply happy to be able to show them how much we valued them. My team understood that I wanted every person to be treated with the dignity and respect of a CEO. Who we are mattered, and what we do needs to reflect who we are. To all our surprise, as we worked late hours following September 11, the cleaning ladies started bringing in homemade food for us to make sure we were eating. It was an amazing example of how kindness begets kindness. These women worked for a private cleaning company for minimum wage, but their humanity was larger than their pocketbook. They pooled their resources in our time of crisis and showered us with their kindness.

AON, as a company, put its people first, took care of families that had lost their loved ones, and put all New York office survivors through months of counseling to do the right thing. In the Celtic language, AON *means oneness*, and the CEO Pat Ryan set the tone for living that value authentically. It is during a crisis that the true character of an organization and its people are revealed. I have had the honor to work for a British bank and a US corporation that valued its people. During times of crisis, these two organizations courageously lived their values and earned the trust of their employees. One could argue that it was a function of time and the indomitable will of the singular leader at the top who set the tone. That may be the case, and we can have that debate at another time and place. But what remains a fact is that organizations can embody humanity and live their value with courage. When we see what is going on in the world today, and I hear people talk about how business, government, and organizations are all bad, I remind them to pause and think about it.

Every organization is comprised of people—be it business, nonprofit, or government. Therefore, if an organization is corrupt, that means the people in that organization are corrupt.

One group may be the corrupt actors, but the remaining who choose to stay silent are equally complicit in that corruption. The Irish Philosopher and Statesman Edmund Burk succinctly stated that *"the only thing necessary for evil to triumph is for good men to do nothing."* We see that today, all over the world.

During my time at AON, I had the honor of having some exceptional individuals on my team. Kas' United Nations was how everyone in the firm referred to my team because we came from all over the world. Tam Vo was my trusted senior finance leader. Andrea and Eva were on Tam's team and made for a fierce trio who ran an efficient operation as the financial business partners for the GMs we served. Clark was our young intern form Illinois State University who was innovative in his ability to solve any problem and could find frugal solutions that never broke the bank. Ryan was our young team addition from North Park University, where I taught, and he proved to be a reliable professional who had a moral compass that could be counted on, regardless of the circumstances. Owen was our University of Wisconsin intern who brought great energy to the team with a work ethic of a mature professional. John was our steady, reliable controller who was the voice of reason. There were other members of the team who also played their part equally well.

We had a team that supported each other and transformed each other as we grew the business. I made sure my team and their families knew how much I valued them. To show my appreciation and gratitude, twice a year, we gathered for a day of food, fun, and celebration as families, once in the summer and then during the Christmas season. Showing my gratitude to not just my team but to their families was vital for me. It was the families that made sacrifices, so my team could be present and impactful. We have all moved on to different organizations and cities for the most part, but we remain connected and make time to celebrate each other's success and happiness. Clark, Ryan, and Owen are leaders in their organizations and their teams. It warms my heart to see the young men remaining true to their own purpose and driving change in their own circles. We all had the opportunity to ennoble each other, and this team will always have one of those special soft spots in my heart!

While I was at AON, I was notified by my immigration attorney retained by AT&T about my citizenship process. Steve had kept his word to the end, to make sure my immigration process was seen through to my US citizenship under his watch, even when he was not my boss. That is the kind of honor, an honor bound by words, that builds trust. He was not an easy man for whom to work. He demanded a lot from you. But he also demanded a lot of himself. Twelve years after entering the US as an international student, I finally became a citizen. **What we seek in the world seeks us in return. When we seek authenticity, courage, and honor, those qualities will seek us. The energy of the universe is fully in tune.**

As AON went through a leadership transition, I was pursued by a global bank in the mortgage industry to help with their technology-based integration of wholesale, retail, and correspondent banking divisions. I accepted the role of senior VP of finance and transitioned into my new role. I had come from a British bank background that balanced its role as the federal reserve for the British colonies while being a for-profit bank. I was trained to put the socio-economic impact front and center in banking decisions because banks, through their credit creation capability, can make or break economies. What I actually saw in my new role did not sit well with me. I tried to negotiate alternate approaches, but the willingness to course-correct was not there. I had a choice to make.

After discussing my concerns with my husband Mike, I decided to speak my truth to the leadership team. I was now older and more mature. So, I approached it as an opportunity to present change. If that failed, I would exit the organization. When I sat down and shared my proposal with my boss, he listened patiently. He and I both knew I had a large sign-on bonus that pays out at the end of the first year, and given the performance of the bank, I had a lucrative year-end performance bonus waiting. He was counting on the fact that money motivated me. I think he thought I was going to vent and then go on and keep doing what I was asked to do because the money was waiting. I, on the other hand, was thinking of karma, socio-economic disaster, and the need to live a life of purpose. My *being* conflicted with what I was being asked to *do*, I asked for three months to explore alternatives and determine the just course of action that provided a win-win resolution. If there was no resolution found at the end of three months, I would leave. I guess my request was not taken seriously.

When the ninety days went by, I returned to my boss to say goodbye. He was rather surprised that I was serious about walking away from the money coming my way shortly. He voiced his thought without giving credence to the looming economic crisis the society was facing if we continued down this path. When he intimated that walking away from money for principles was a stupid decision, I could not let it go. This was another one of those moments of waving the red cloth in front of the bull in my professional life. *I must have been a Spanish bullfighter in my last life,* I thought to myself as I prepared to respond.

"Do I look like a prostitute?" were the words that rolled out of my mouth.

He was totally shocked by my comeback and said, "Why in the world would you say something like that?" It was not my nature to speak that way, and I took him by total surprise.

I calmly said, "If you know that I would never sell my body, what makes you think I would sell my soul?" That was the last time I set foot in that bank. I quit my job that day, started my own private practice, and enrolled in a PhD program with the explicit purpose of researching the nexus of profits and ethics. This world needed some balance, and I was going to make my pet peeve a part of my life's purpose.

One might ask, how can this situation and those in it ennoble me? To my way of thinking, they created an environment where I had to become introspective and make choices to remain true to myself. **They ennobled me by giving me an opportunity to choose how I wanted to show up in the world. They helped me, unknowingly, to become a better version of me. I have learned that it is not just positive situations that help bring out what is noble in each one of us.** When we were growing up, my father had a house rule. When one or two us did something wrong, all four of us got punished. No amount of arguing was going to sway him, and one day, I demanded an explanation. He told all of us that we are each responsible for what the rest of us do because, in life, actions of one have consequences for all. If the hotheaded boys wanted to do something bad, it was the role of us girls to find a way to stop them from going through with it. He would make us each get a branch from our guava tree, clean all the leaves, and put oil on the switch. Then we each got beaten by the switch we had made for the occasion. After a couple of these so-called life lessons, I decided not to have any more of it. If it took tying my brother to a tree to keep them out of trouble, I just did so. **I know this could be shocking to the US reader, but the lesson we learned has stayed with me. It is ingrained in me to step up and speak truth to power because the actions of a few have consequences for all of us.**

Negative situations have that same opportunity for ennobling us if we allowed. People who make our lives miserable teach us too. Horrible circumstances are better teachers than good ones because lasting learning happens when we are uncomfortable. Looking back at life, if not for the civil war and all the challenges that life presented, I wouldn't have emerged as I am today. I am grateful for the bad because it strengthened me and taught me to appreciate the good. It taught me how to even recognize the good! I am often asked if I could change one thing about my life, what would I change, and my answer every time is *not a single thing*. Every one of those things together made me who I am today. Every person and situation ennobled me because I allowed every human interaction to be a teachable and learnable moment to create an opportunity for my transformation. I stand before you as the sum total of my life experience, and I am yet transforming.

A few months after I exited the mortgage banking world, the sub-prime crisis crippled the global economy—what I feared had happened. There were winners, and there were losers. I continued to learn from those around me. Writing to publish, completing my PhD in finance, teaching graduate school, and serving my clients kept me busy. At home, **Mike and I had peace because I had chosen to live an authentic life to allow my soul to be free and visible. We both had started from nothing, and now we had each other. We could take on the world because we had each other.** This change in my career trajectory proved to be the best choice, but we did not know it then. We have a compelling need to live our truth.

My consulting practice thrived, and I was hired to help organizations effectively navigate their restructuring. Each of these engagements led to three- to five-year engagements within those organizations. Being the VP of continuous improvement for a for-profit multi-university system to prepare them for the upcoming regulatory standards and being a CFO for a twenty-billion-dollar pension fund that was less than 50 percent funded to negotiate state government regulation changes, along with modernization to assure its long-term viability, were two of the impactful assignments I had undertaken.

I currently work for Berkshire Hathaway's new acquisition, Duracell. The battery company stand-up was my original assignment nearly five years ago when Warren Buffet purchased it from P&G. Post-stand-up, I was asked to stay on to drive continuous improvement and process simplification to unleash the deal value. Over time, this role has evolved into building the global learning and development organization and integrate an appropriate curriculum that works for in-person as well as remote learning.

All the relationships I had invested in, my students, my team members, my strategic partners, and just random professionals who had heard me speak or read what I had published, continued to grow. I can connect organizations with talented young people, pair up young people with integrity to have impactful mentors, and build bridges to make good come to life. These are not things that are done for money. They are done to fulfill the soul. These are win-win opportunity creations at a time and place where everyone is feeling lost and left behind. **This is a long way from a childhood in a civil war, but there are parallels and *deja vu* moments. The constant thread remains that what is done to us and our circumstances do not define us. It is up to us to turn each obstacle into stepping-stones to success. The conduit to make that success possible is our ability to build authentic relationships.**

LESSONS LEARNED:

➢ *Do not let a job be the reason to turn your back on your authentic self.* The job should never define us. The job should be the vehicle to let your soul become visible to make meaningful change.

➢ *Organizations do not harm people. People harm people.* Organizations, be it business, government, or nonprofit, are merely names, logos, and addresses without its people. So, if we want social justice and equity to address structural issues, influence change through the people. If change is not possible, staying on and profiting from it makes that person harmful to others.

➢ *Our word is our bond.* When we keep our word on little things, we build trust to accomplish big things. Giving our word is giving our honor and failing to keep our word makes for a dishonorable person. Therefore, talking to talk is a slow march toward professional suicide.

CHAPTER 12

LIGHTING THE LAMP

"It is better to light one small candle
than to curse the darkness."
—Confucius

Continuous improvement is not just a concept for process and business. It is a valuable approach to life itself. We know that the only constant in life is change, and therefore, our ability to continually change and be adaptable is what gives us resiliency to live a meaningful life. This change cannot happen in a vacuum. It must take place in the context of our socio-economic realities at the intersection of the transformation of each person. Take a moment and imagine if I am the only one who pursued a specific field and mastered it. Will I be able to benefit from that knowledge if no one else understood it or saw the usefulness of it? The answer is no. Therefore, I need to take others along for the journey of understanding, so when I offer my special knowledge, others know what it is, how to receive it, and how to put it to use. This simple illustration shows me that my continued improvement needs to happen as part of a larger collaborative process. I do not live, grow, and thrive alone.

Have you ever thought of what keeps a knife sharp? Using it is what keeps it sharp. The human mind, heart, and body are the same way. A sedentary state is not healthy for the whole person. Exercise and activity are not just for the body. They have to be for the heart and mind, too. I cannot, for the life of me, imagine actively engaging my heart, mind, and body solely toward myself. I would not know what that would be like. The only sane and rational way to do so is to engage with others, **sharing ideas, and debating constructively to expand the thinking. Showing kindness to another person and finding joy in it, the willingness to accept help from someone to grow in an area of life, or taking a walk alongside someone and sharing the moment are all things we do naturally. So, why assume our growth and success cannot organically happen this same way by engaging our heart, mind, and body so the soul could live its purpose?**

This line of thinking has guided me over the years, and my journey has proven the immense value the approach brings to everyone along the way. It is novel in a society that looks for material value in all things and approaches every human interaction as a transaction. The question people ask before agreeing to meet someone is, "What can you give me that is useful for me today?" The question employers ask employees is, "What have you done to improve the bottom line today?" Are these the right questions? What are these questions telling us about who we are? Is this what I want to be defined by? **It is true that we live in a disposable society but look at all the harm it has caused our environment. Look at the toxicity it has created for other creatures, both on land and in the sea? Should we really take this disposable concept and make**

it the baseline for human relationships and interactions? This is a series of introspective questions I ask myself as I process the world around me. The answer I come up with is, "No, I need to be the change that breaks this toxic cycle."

Deciding to break the cycle is the easy part. How to do it is the real challenge. In the book, SWITCH: *How to change things when change is hard,* authors Chip Heath and Dan Heath explore the concept in an easy-to-understand manner. This is one of my go-to resources to bring about change in an organization or society. As previously noted in an earlier chapter, the authors illustrate leading change as riding the elephant. Unlike riding a horse, one cannot tell the elephant where to go or what to do. The success of riding an elephant lies in motivating the elephant to want to go where transformation resides. Bringing about organizational change in business or government is challenging enough. How can I then take the lessons learned in business and engage a global society? Can I start with my sphere of influence and gently expand that circle of influence?

All the pondering was of no value until I did it. I have the voice of Yoda telling me, "Do or do not. There is no try!" Who knew a little puppet character in a sci-fi movie could take up permanent residence in my head? I took a leap of faith and decided to take up VoiceAmerica on the offer they had been making me for a few months to host my own radio show. They were trying to get me to do a business show. **I negotiated and arranged to do an empowerment show. My show was named "Unleash your Inner Goldilocks: *How to Get It Just Right!*"** I wanted a playful and non-threatening entry point into empowerment with a focus on centeredness and balance.

Goldilocks symbolizes balance. Not being extreme on either end of any issue spectrum, finding the centeredness, and leading from the middle toward goal attainment is the message embodied in Goldilocks. I picked this centeredness as the pathway for empowerment. **Successful individuals, families, organizations, and countries lead from the middle**

with the firm grasp of this inner balance. When one leads from that centered position, the sphere of influence has seven degrees of impact: three levels right and left of the center and those in the center. Compare this to someone who tries to lead from one of the extremes with only a single direction of influence. Therefore, "Getting it just right" is a balanced transformational pursuit. It is the optimal way to collaborate and bring about lasting change for shared prosperity. I was applying the learning from my doctoral dissertation to design my radio show, keeping in mind that I was riding an elephant.

The radio show took off, and I was building an international following with rich content and vibrant guests who engaged in discussions to find the centered approach for solving everyday problems in life. There was a pent-up demand for this shared journey, and I was given the opportunity to ennoble others. I continue to teach, publish, and present at professional conferences to effectively balance good governance for individuals, organizations, and society to strike a win-win-win balance. These were avenues I was able to spread my opportunity to ennoble others. **The secret is that the more I focused on passing on the good and bringing out the noble qualities in others, the more fulfilling my life became. Goodness can be just as contagious as diseases and toxicity. The greater incremental goodness we put out into the world, the greater the opportunity to get to the tipping point needed for lasting positive change.** The lamp I was lighting to brighten the path of others was brightening my path, too. I believe **the human being was not created as a transactional creature. We were created to be transformational at our core. How else could we explain evolution?**

As I continued balancing my various interests, I started synthesizing to learn from the intersectionality of business and social viability. Jay Barney's sustainable competitive advantage theory focusses on how to build a viable business that is capable of sustained, long-term economic benefits. I started thinking of repurposing this for building sustainable, long-term economic benefits for society. What would that model look like? I have developed this model over time as I have helped build various social initiatives and nonprofits, applying this blueprint to guide my strategic guidance behind the scenes. This has been my frame of reference to help bring initiatives to life. The VRIO Elements and Economic Underpinning come from Jay Barney, where the acronym stands for **V**aluable, **R**are, **I**mitable, and **O**rganizationally based. The goal here is to ascertain if the services provide value to the society, unique enough to command the attention and social demand, difficult to be replicated, and therefore hold societal attention, and built on a firm foundation of organizational culture to capture socio-economic value.

Social Transformation Journey

Social Application Question for Growth & Empowerment

How do we develop the HUMAN POTENTIAL to CREATE SOCIAL VALUE and how do we get the BUY IN to start the TRANSFORMATIONAL JOURNEY?

How do we differentiate and collaborate to reach parity with other communities that enjoy normal economic performance integrating TRUST?

How do we build RESILIENCY to cultivate adaptability and ability to evolve as the internal and external environments change?

How do we integrate ENNOBLING to build a CULTURE of SHARED PROSPERITY to organically remain sustainable?

How do we TRANSFORM our society into a SELF HEALING ECO-SYSTEM to CONTINUALLY THRIVE?

Adapted applying Jay Barney's VRIO Analysis for
Ennobled for Success © by Dr. Kasthuri Henry

Organizational culture is the unique ingredient that makes sustainability possible. No amount of strategy can make an organization successful if the right culture is absent. Peter Drucker, the father of strategy, aptly stated that "organizational culture can eat strategy for breakfast, lunch, and dinner" when not instilled and cultivated right. All this translates from business to nonprofit and society. A society's culture gives it viability. Keeping that in mind, I have developed my

Social Transformation Journey map presented above and will continue to refine through the learnings as initiatives are implemented.

I have had the opportunity to mentor and shape the path of many over the years, including students of all ages and young people in the community. Foreign students like Hao and Joyston, who came into my life as my students, then stayed on to blossom into wonderful young adults finding their purpose and making their mark in the US. They have become an extension of the family, and it is amazing to see them paying forward the gift of ennobling they have received. **I engage my students in volunteer activities as part of their social interaction and leadership development by serving others. Lasting leadership comes from the desire to serve and not the ego to control.** Taking my students though this journey has been a fulfilling part of life. Not all of them take to it, but those who do, find their purpose and professional fulfillment. When they do, they master the art of gratitude, kindness, and compassion that continues to be their guiding light. They also turn around and help the next group take that transformational journey.

My public safety and homeland security students have partnered with me to take their learning in the class-room to drive meaningful social change. Fire Chief Spain of Bensenville, Illinois, and Fire Chief Gilgenberg of Burbank, Illinois, have helped organize community CPR lessons and community engagement events to unite the members of the community through caring service engagements. Deputy Fire Chief Decker of Waukegan partnered with me on an intern-ship program where graduate students had the opportunity to do an internship with the fire department for reasonable pay and got the experience to translate classroom learning into public-sector work application. Karen was one of my graduate students who successfully completed her internship and secured a government job upon graduation. The intern-ship program was a win-win-win collaboration where Karen gained work experience, while the fire department got their planning, budgeting, and monthly close process automated without a high dollar investment, and the taxpayers benefitted from the outcome. I got to plan, coordinate, and manage the internship outside of my scope of work as my contribution to the society that has given me my adopted home. **These have been win-win-win partnerships where individuals in society, organizations like the fire department, and the taxpaying society have all benefited with no one having to be at the losing end of a deal.**

The Chicago EMS students, who are predominantly women, have been another group that is collaborating to build bridges and find that centered balance. Ambulance Commander Kuprianczyk has gone from being a student to a dear friend and collaborator I can count on. Some like Firefighter Lockett of Chicago, Illinois, and Division Chief Schum of Truckee Meadows, have been inspired to pursue higher education to empower future generations of public safety professionals giving me the honor to be in their continued educational journey. Countless others have gone on to put their learning into shaping the profession and grooming the next generation. There is nothing more satisfying than getting updates from former students or partnering with them on bringing about the social change we need in our communities.

The US military students have transitioned into private-sector careers, taking with them their skills and leadership to transform their own lives and the lives of those in their private-sector organizations. Some have even taken the leap of faith and started their own business, putting the data analysis and financial knowledge into entrepreneurial pursuits. **All these endeavors have afforded the opportunity to cross-pollinate government, private, and nonprofit sectors to create an awareness of how interconnected we all are. Communities cannot choose one of the three sectors and villainize the remaining. A viable society needs all three sectors to be carefully synchronized with the households if transformation is to take place.** It is all about carefully taking the baby steps to ride the elephant.

The students who thought they could take advantage of the support system that gave them the opportunity to then kick down the ladder that helped them may have had momentary benefits by stepping on others, but time has been their best teacher and leveler. They have learned the hard way that the toes they stepped on to climb the ladder are connected to the butts they must kiss as they found themselves in a pickle.

Children of my network from all over the world are also an important group of young people who enrich my life today. They are in this country for education with no parents or family to guide them. Having taken that journey myself, I am acutely aware of the burdens these young folks carry. Being there for them in the capacity of a host family is a beautiful way for my family to give back. The recent US immigration drama and inconsistent policy-making without thinking through the ramifications have kept us all busy exploring alternatives. In a manner of speaking, the recent turn of events with the pandemic and immigration visa process dramas have given me the opportunity to teach these young students the need for resiliency and master the art of building resiliency while grasping the need for scaling and being agile. They are learning how to thrive in spite of the adversities. Anoop in California and Michael in Arizona are both sons of women who worked with me at the bank. Strategizing with their mothers, planning the options, and watching them execute the options with the maturity of professional adults is a joy. **The power structure that thinks they are destroying the opportunities of international students is helping all these students by making them transform, become resilient, and laser-focus with a purpose to fulfill their own life promise.**

Marquell was a young man I met at a community award ceremony, and we made an instant connection. His natural curiosity, propensity to dissect problems to find the root cause, and then find novel ways to solve them was talent that was worth harnessing. He had the potential for great things, and a "can do" attitude tempered with optimism. Marquell and I have taken a mentor-mentee journey over the last four to five years. While his big dream will be revealed at the right time, his current work is focused on building **Pure Alchemy, a non-profit organization that works to meet tomorrow's needs, today, through young adults.** I have been placed in a position to guide Marquell and his team of young alchemists through this journey as a member of the board. We have brought a couple of experienced professionals to help in the building, knowing that over time, the transformation will occur when the young alchemists are ready to step up and take on those roles.

Pure Alchemy uses music and creative arts to bring community members together. We also collaborate with Unity Partnership, a local nonprofit, and the founder, Regina Brent, focuses on building a positive relationship between law enforcement and minorities. Raise Vibrations is the music event we run in park districts to adhere to the CDC guidelines during the pandemic when the conditions are suitable for outdoor gatherings. **The need to build a cohesive society is important now, more so than ever. To be able to work side by side with young men and women of all races to build a future they need to see is a special one.**

I take the opportunity to use my show as an amplifier to host important conversations. How do we understand the root cause to solve our problems from a balanced perspective for a meaningful win-win outcome? How do we effectively self-promote and network to fulfill our purpose? How do we eliminate negative self-talk and grow with self-awareness and social awareness to fulfill our purpose? How do we build meaningful relationships with ourselves and others to bring about lasting change? How do we recognize bias and microaggression to then transform ourselves and our society to bring lasting social progress? These are some of the conversations we are having on the show with participant engagement from the US, Asia, Latin America, and the Caribbean. These issues are not unique to one country. They are social and personal development opportunities for all of us.

As others have ennobled me to make my life possible, I must continue to ennoble others. The beauty of this process is that every life I get to touch touches my life too. My mom used to always say, "As *one lamp lights another, nobleness enkindles nobleness.*" I do not know the source of wisdom, but it is one of those messages that has stayed with me. I am a believer that our soul lives on through the lives we transform, and we each leave a part of our energy with those we share this transformational journey. My definition of success is peace and happiness. What could bring about more peace and happiness than building to last and ennobling for success?

LESSONS LEARNED:

- ➤ **Social change does not happen by accident.** Various parts of the community must come together to bring about purposeful change, and the first step to accomplishing it is respectful dialogue to build trust. It is only with trust that we have the chance to craft win-win solutions.

- ➤ **Passing the torch and ennobling others is an important aspect of building to last.** If we do not work together to leave this world better than we found it, have we not just taken up space and time?

- ➤ **Gratitude is the fertilizer that helps cultivate flourishing relationships that build self-healing ecosystems that make sustainability possible.** Nature provides the blueprint for what a viable ecosystem looks and feels like. By being aware of ourselves and our surroundings, we must take the time to gratefully replicate what mother nature has generously gifted us: an ecosystem that has sustained us, even when we have not appreciated her.

CLOSING THOUGHTS

This book, through storytelling, strives to bring about the centeredness necessary for the most important journey of each of our lives: **the journey within ourselves for the purpose of self-reflection, cultivate self-aware, learn to self-manage and build the keystone relationship for life success**, the relationship with our own soul to connect with the being we each are. This is not a one and done trip down memory lane. **It is a continually transforming journey that is expected to help the reader become the constant gardener of their purposeful life fertilized by gratitude to grow a colorful garden of life filled with ennobled flowers. Kindness, compassion, empathy, and other noble qualities in us will only flourish if we give it away.** Hoarding them serves absolutely no purpose.

Keeping a gratitude journal, as noted in the introduction, is a good starting point to embark on the journey to become ennobled. It is important for the journal to capture both good and bad experiences to understand how each of them can give us different perspectives to aid in our personal transformation. Equally important is the need to ask the question, "Why?" Why was that particular situation a valuable point of reference? What was the teachable and learnable opportunity contained within it? How can that opportunity bring out a noble quality? How do we get past the hurt and trauma of the moment to see the gift of that experience and embrace the gift of transformation? These are vital questions to ponder in order to shape a meaningful path forward. Such an approach has the power of moving a person from being a victim to becoming the driver of their own destiny.

As the journey within is undertaken, it is imperative that feelings and emotions are acknowledged, and the intensity understood to find the lasting value emerging from each experience. It does not mean the experience is forgotten. It means the experience no longer has the power to control choices and resulting consequences. It is at this point of inner freedom that wisdom and insights emerge. When one reaches this place, neither anger, fear, nor sorrow drive choices. Thoughtful and pragmatic positivity is the guiding light. Such a journey of self-discovery is better undertaken with a support system. There are plans in the works to bring that support system and tools forward.

Following the release of this book, The Gratitude Journal will be released as a fifty-two-week writing journal to help facilitate the transformational journey of those who choose to adopt this ennobled road to success. Thereafter, additional compilation of Lessons Learned, the Road Map for the Ennobling Journey, and the launch of Ennobled for Success Community can be expected. To stay connected and engage with the community committed to ennobling, sign up at https://kashenry.com/EnnobledForSuccess/. Join the movement and build a firm foundation today for your successes tomorrow.

ABOUT THE AUTHOR

Dr. Kasthuri Henry, PhD, is driven by her mission of **Building to Last and Ennobling for Success**. Her ability to understand the importance of first developing the **being,** and then bringing that authentic self to all the **doing,** makes her a sought-after member of Forbes' Coaches Council. She is a compassionate human being who believes everyone should have the opportunity to fulfill their life's purpose and live an authentic life fearlessly with the right to not be defined by a single story. She is an accomplished professional who trains organizations and coaches individuals around the world to grow with mindfulness, demonstrating good governance to balance the interest of the individual, organization, and society for sustained mutual prosperity. Dr. Kas has successfully led global transformation as a financial strategist, CFO, and change agent across Fortune-500 companies. As a graduate school professor at North Park University and Southern Illinois University, she continues to transform students representing the US military, US public safety and homeland security, private sector, and nonprofit sectors.

A centered approach to solving life's challenges is the theme of her weekly podcast, **"Unleash your Inner Goldilocks: How to get it just right!"**

Social Media links

Facebook: https://www.facebook.com/DrKasHenry

LinkedIn: https://www.linkedin.com/in/dr-kasthuri-henry-phd-mba-ctp-6-sigma-black-belt-2028b06/

Twitter: https://twitter.com/DrKasthuri

Instagram: https://www.instagram.com/henrykasthuri/

YouTube: https://www.youtube.com/channel/UCtZZPdBCo_OTyccJLqEJc-A

ENDNOTES

i. New World Encyclopedia, https://www.newworldencyclopedia.org/entry/Dravidian_peoples.

ii. World Atlas, https://www.worldatlas.com/articles/oldest-languages-still-in-use-today.html.

iii. Encyclopedia Britannica, https://www.britannica.com/place/Sri-Lanka/British-Ceylon-1796-1900.

iv. Ibid.

1. Tamil the oldest language: *World Atlas*, https://www.worldatlas.com/articles/oldest-languages-still-in-use-today.html.

2. 70% Non-Verbal Communication Stats: Hull, Raymond H. PhD. "The Art of Nonverbal Communication in Practice." *The Hearing Journal*: May 2016 - Volume 69 - Issue 5 - p 22,24. doi: 10.1097/01.HJ.0000483270.59643.cc. https://journals.lww.com/thehearingjournal/Fulltext/2016/05000/The_Art_of_Nonverbal_Communication_in_Practice.5.aspx.

3. Gandhi shaping MLK and Mandela's approaches: https://www.bartleby.com/essay/Mohandas-Gandhi-Nelson-Mandela-and-Martin-Luther-F3VMM84J8MRS.

4. Kasturi in Ayurvedic Medicine, Medicine of last resort: https://www.easyayurveda.com/2018/01/01/kasturi-musk-deer-kasthuri-kastoori/.

5. Sri Lankan Colonial Reference of Portuguese, Dutch & English:https://en.vikidia.org/wiki/Colonization_of_Sri_Lanka.

6. Srirmavo. Bandaranayake: https://www.britannica.com/biography/Sirimavo-Bandaranaike

7. Dissertation Published: Henry, K. (2011). A quantitative analysis of ethical leadership character traits and moral cognition among chief financial officer (CFO) leadership teams. ProQuest LLC, ISBN: 1124450815 (ISBN-13: 9781124450810; ISBN: 9781124450810).

8. Chip Heath & Dan Heath (2010). Switch: How to Change Things When Change Is Hard.

REVIEWS

"This autobiography is a gem from start to finish. It tells the story of one woman's journey from an extremely difficult and dangerous childhood, to an accomplished and centered woman of major influence in our world. Time and again, Kas shows how it is possible to weather the vicissitudes of life, no matter how extreme or unfair, and turn them into positive energy to ennoble the future. At the end of each chapter, she gives three lessons learned, so the book is easy to digest and apply to our own life. When describing this book, the word 'inspirational' is inadequate."
   —Bob Whipple, "The Trust Ambassador," MBA CPTD, CEO Leadergrow, Inc.
   https://leadergrow.com/

"Ennobled for Success is a must-read book for organizations, leaders and conscious people who believe in creating their lives rather than choosing victim roles and for those who strive for integrity and ethics in all their endeavors. Throughout the book, you can feel the presence of Dr. Kas and her own remarkable essence, which is full of grace, gratitude, kindness, strength, and bravery. She and her life story become ennobling catalysts for those who are lucky enough to read this book."
   —Dr. Marina Kostina, CEO & Founder of Ravenous Life Healing Center. Bestselling Author, Hypnotherapist, Coach and Energy Healer

"Ennobled for Success is already one of the greatest gifts of the decade, offering exhilarating story-telling and fascinating 'chin check moments' for the student in all of us. The teachable moments are plentiful and each deep dive is very poignant. However, the real call to action is when Dr. Kas asks us to listen 'to our inner self and those around us because we all impact each other.' If this book is to hit your eyesight, consider your higher self provoked to shed a layer of baggage while getting ready to accept responsibility for your own growth."
—Marquell Oliver, Founder of Pure Alchemy
https://www.thepurealchemygroup.com

"This is a heartfelt and transparent 'love letter' to those who feel they are not good enough. Dr. Henry selflessly shares her experiences addressing the damaging impact of judging a person based on things such as skin color and gender. Ennobled for Success is more than the story of a woman who battled stereotypes and 'old ways of thinking' instilled in her as a young girl to successfully become a CFO. It inspires us to understand we are a 'being' first with a purpose; our job or career is not part of the formula that gives us our true value."
—Traci S. Campbell, CEO & Founder, BIBO Worldwide, LLC & The BIBO Foundation.
www.biboweekly.com.

"Kasthuri Henry authentically weaves her powerful life experiences into her business success. She crosses the chasm between war-torn persecuted Sri Lankan and successful, polished US business executive, making her the perfect choice to craft a future vision incorporating multi-levels and facets of society."
—Charlotte Allen, CEO, International Bestselling Author, Speaker
www.rebelsuccessforleaders.com

"With Ennobled for Success, Kas generously shares her life-lessons, extensive knowledge, and diverse experiences, inspiring us, while giving us a roadmap, to be the best that we can be. Speaking to us about her own very human journey, she draws us in with compelling universal lessons on living a principled life of integrity, authenticity, mindfulness, resilience, compassion, kindness, hope, friendship, love, and an unwavering belief in the essential goodness of humanity. A must-read for all who aspire to live this one life fully and without regret."
    —Dr. Susila Kulasingam, Pharmaceutical Physician Executive and long-time friend.

"Ennobled for Success is a powerful book where every word hits home, making one self-reflect on their own life journey. The book is filled with rich language to make us understand our own purpose in life, as we visualize what Dr. Kasthuri is trying to convey through her powerful journey of living her dreams. This book will surely motivate those who feel they have not embarked on their journey of self-discovery life could have some surprising results for them."
    —Rennu Dhillon D.S.c., Founder - Genius Kids & Win With Words, Author and Motivational Speaker

"Dr. Henry provides you with a powerful presentation through the written word of her life's journey decisions based on ethics, equality, cultural diversification via respect and guidance to mankind, resilience, friendships, and education to everyone who is blessed to come in contact with her. Dr. Henry is a trustful humanitarian who cultivates her garden of life through her selfless love of other individuals' success. THIS BOOK IS A MUST-READ AND RE-READ!!!"
    —Fire Chief Michael F. Spain, MA (Retired), Bensenville Fire Protection District,
    https://www.linkedin.com/in/mike-spain-6835a514/

"Ennobled for Success is must-read guide that will unleash the potential of any leader with the intention of reaching higher. Dr. Kasthuri Henry has captured all the elements beautifully on every page."
—Jacqueline Camacho-Ruiz, 21x Author, International Speaker, Entrepreneur, Pilot

"Ennobled for Success reminded me to be me, again. In a business world where one is so easily lost in the rat race it is easy to be swept away. I have never read a book and felt as grounded in my authentic self, valuing kindness and lifting up others, as I did from reading this book. The reader takes an intimate journey of self-discovery and strength. Emotions are brought forth as a phoenix rises through the ashes, giving permission to be unapologetically confident that a rising tide lifts all boats, thus giving us all opportunities to find the good in any situation, in any person, and in any time."
—Tara DeGrace,
https://www.linkedin.com/in/taradegrace/

"Dr. Kas has created an inspirational book that is also an instructional manual on how to achieve success without losing sight of one's values and principles. She provides a model for those strive to serve society while holding onto important beliefs and ideals. If you get to read this story of a feisty young girl spanning her life from a civil war to a US CFO, consider yourself to be fortunate. She makes us believe that we can each develop the necessary noble qualities to attain our success by committing to the process of embracing gratitude to be ennobled!"
—Ruchira Palliyaguru, International Cricket Umpire, Sri Lanka Cricket and International Cricket Council
ruchirapalliyaguru@gmail.com

"It's clear from the outset that Dr. Henry's rich and culture-filled life journey has cultivated many powerful and long-lasting teaching moments we could all benefit from. In our present day and age, it is more important than ever that leadership needs to be held accountable to develop and spread noble qualities. Well worth the read."
—Patrick Haddad, CEO Oopgo Inc, Forbes Tech Council Expert Advisor, and USMC Veteran
https://www.linkedin.com/in/haddadpatrick/

"Ennobled for Success will help you lean into your truth, your beliefs, and teach you how to hack into your own best self. As a world-renowned expert profiler who understands how people are wired, I recognize Dr. Kasthuri's brilliance in helping you go deeper to bring the best of you forward."
—Susan Ibitz, Human Behavior Hacker, Human Behavior Lab.
https://humanbehaviorlab.com/

"In her delightful book, Dr. Kas takes you on a journey of discovery of her life's purpose. These stories are at times funny, painful, exciting, and sad, but they are all full of valuable life lessons. These lessons are very applicable to private business, public organizations, and the military, because they deal with one common denominator: extraordinary people. As you read this book, you will learn how gratitude, kindness, compassion, and empathy unlock a successful, meaningful, and ennobled life. Students, teachers, and business leaders will all benefit from the delightful fruits of knowledge that grow in Dr Kas' garden."
—Wolfgang Trampe, Human Resources Leader, Duracell (A Berkshire Hathaway Company), Latin America.
https://www.linkedin.com/in/wolfgangtrampe/

"True to form, Dr. Henry is honest, sincere, vulnerable, and genuine as she shares her introspective journey to becoming a successful person and leader. While some use fables, Kas shares real-life experiences to give us perspective and lessons to learn on how being authentic, caring, and purpose-driven can bring success. Public and private sector leadership should take this as a gut check to reset to what is important. We should all spend more time being grateful and learning to guide the elephant rather than eat it."

—Joe Schum, Division Chief – Truckee Meadows Fire & Rescue, Reno, NV and International Public Safety Leadership Ethics Institute (IPSLEI) Board Member. https://www.ipslei.org/

Made in the USA
Columbia, SC
28 October 2020

23674166R00104